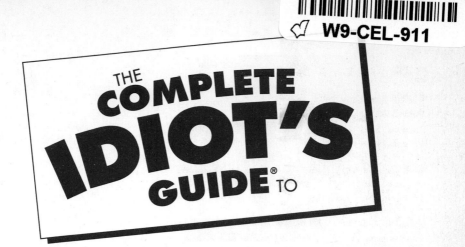

Branding Yourself

by Sherry Beck Paprocki and Ray Paprocki

ALPHA

A member of Penguin Group (USA) Inc.

To Ana and Justin

ALPHA BOOKS

Published by the Penguin Group

Penguin Group (USA) Inc., 375 Hudson Street, New York, New York 10014, USA

Penguin Group (Canada), 90 Eglinton Avenue East, Suite 700, Toronto, Ontario M4P 2Y3, Canada (a division of Pearson Penguin Canada Inc.)

Penguin Books Ltd., 80 Strand, London WC2R 0RL, England

Penguin Ireland, 25 St. Stephen's Green, Dublin 2, Ireland (a division of Penguin Books Ltd.)

Penguin Group (Australia), 250 Camberwell Road, Camberwell, Victoria 3124, Australia (a division of Pearson Australia Group Pty. Ltd.)

Penguin Books India Pvt. Ltd., 11 Community Centre, Panchsheel Park, New Delhi—110 017, India

Penguin Group (NZ), 67 Apollo Drive, Rosedale, North Shore, Auckland 1311, New Zealand (a division of Pearson New Zealand Ltd.)

Penguin Books (South Africa) (Pty.) Ltd., 24 Sturdee Avenue, Rosebank, Johannesburg 2196, South Africa

Penguin Books Ltd., Registered Offices: 80 Strand, London WC2R 0RL, England

Copyright © 2009 by Sherry Beck Paprocki and Ray Paprocki

International Standard Book Number: 978-1-59257-896-2
Library of Congress Catalog Card Number: 2008941487

11 10 09   8 7 6 5 4 3 2 1

Interpretation of the printing code: The rightmost number of the first series of numbers is the year of the book's printing; the rightmost number of the second series of numbers is the number of the book's printing. For example, a printing code of 09-1 shows that the first printing occurred in 2009.

Printed in the United States of America

Note: This publication contains the opinions and ideas of its authors. It is intended to provide helpful and informative material on the subject matter covered. It is sold with the understanding that the authors and publisher are not engaged in rendering professional services in the book. If the reader requires personal assistance or advice, a competent professional should be consulted.

The authors and publisher specifically disclaim any responsibility for any liability, loss, or risk, personal or otherwise, which is incurred as a consequence, directly or indirectly, of the use and application of any of the contents of this book.

Most Alpha books are available at special quantity discounts for bulk purchases for sales promotions, premiums, fund-raising, or educational use. Special books, or book excerpts, can also be created to fit specific needs.

For details, write: Special Markets, Alpha Books, 375 Hudson Street, New York, NY 10014.

Publisher: *Marie Butler-Knight*
Editorial Director: *Mike Sanders*
Senior Managing Editor: *Billy Fields*
Acquisitions Editor: *Karyn Gerhard*
Development Editor: *Jennifer Moore*
Senior Production Editor: *Megan Douglass*
Copy Editor: *Michael Dietsch*

Cartoonist: *Steve Barr*
Cover Designer: *Bill Thomas*
Book Designer: *Trina Wurst*
Indexer: *Heather McNeill*
Layout: *Ayanna Lacey*
Proofreader: *John Etchison*

Contents at a Glance

Part 1: **What Is Branding?** 1

1 Personal Branding Defined 3
Building a personal brand requires an honest assessment of yourself.

2 Writing Your Own Branding Story 11
Why let someone else determine your brand? Gain the necessary tools to define yourself.

3 Reaching Your Target Audience 27
Acquiring a deep knowledge about your field and figuring out who you need to impress to reach your goals.

4 Communicating Over the Clutter 39
Sound advice on getting your word out, including the elements of good design.

Part 2: **Launching Your Personal Brand** 49

5 Brand Identity: Starting with Your Resumé 51
Developing a strategy to win over prospective employers.

6 Effective Messaging: Creating Collateral 65
Examining the kinds of marketing materials you'll need to communicate your personal brand to the target audience.

7 Developing Brand Associations 75
Exploring ways to strengthen your personal brand by building relationships.

8 The Total Experience: Living Your Brand 85
Ways to make a good impression, from manners to body language.

Part 3:   Branding in a Modern World   97

9 Mainstream Media Still Counts   99
Why traditional media outlets are important in developing a personal brand. Tips on becoming a one-person media machine.

10 Understanding Public Relations   109
Getting the necessary tools to launch a plan to promote your personal brand.

11 Branding Yourself Via the Web   121
Learn about designing a website, podcasting, electronic newsletters, and more.

12 Personal Communication in a New Age   133
Tips on communicating on social networking sites such as Facebook and MySpace, etiquette for texting, background on blogging, and choosing the electronic tools that suit your personal brand.

13 Should You Buy the Mad Ad, Men?   145
How advertising can elevate your personal brand.

14 Guerilla Tactics in a Noisy World   157
Using creativity to market your brand inexpensively.

Part 4:   Brand Extension and Evolution   169

15 If You Brand It, They Will Come   171
Creating new products based on your core personal brand.

16 Lessons from Megabrand Personalities   181
Case studies of Tiger Woods, Madonna, Oprah Winfrey, Donald Trump, Barack Obama, John McCain, Ralph Lauren, and Ellen DeGeneres.

17 Global Responsibility   189
How to build a personal brand in an international arena while avoiding cultural pitfalls.

18 The Smoke and Fog of Branding   199
    What causes personal brands to go bad?
    Realize the importance of authenticity and
    transparency in a hyper-connected world.

19 Being Your Own Brand Barista   207
    Managing your personal brand is just as
    vital as establishing it. Tips on keeping your
    brand consistent and trustworthy.

20 Branding in the Future   219
    Preparing your personal brand for change,
    and why social responsibility matters.

Appendixes

A Glossary   229
B Resources   235
   Index   239

Contents

Part 1: What Is Branding?   1

1 Personal Branding Defined   3

Personal Branding Defined 4
Who Needs a Personal Brand? 4
Figuring Out Your Brand 5
What Branding Is Not 6
Celebrity Brands 7
Brand Loyalty 8
How to Assess Yourself 9
Be an Expert 9
Managing Your Brand 9

2 Writing Your Own Branding Story   11

Brand Authenticity 12
Know Yourself 13
Get Real for Your Personal Brand 13
Building Your Brand Is Work 14
Why Write Your Branding Story Now? 14
It's About Your Reputation 16
Ask Yourself Some Questions 17
Create a Personal Branding Statement 18
Elaborate 19
Ask for Input from Others 19
Writing Your Branding Story 20
*Summarizing Your Branding Story into
an Elevator Pitch* 22
Balancing Your Brand 23
Brand Perception 23
Brand Positioning 24
Your Brand Positioning Statement 25

3 Reaching Your Target Audience   27

Examining the Needs of Your Target Audience 28
Differentiation: Do You Have Functional
Advantages? 29

Depth of Knowledge 30
Forging an Emotional Bond 31
Relating to Your Audience 33
Brand Messaging 33
  Evolving Needs in the Marketplace 33
  Be an Expert 34
Two Ways to Connect 35
Create Trust... 35

4 Communicating Over the Clutter   39

The Struggle to Get Noticed 40
  Talk to Your Audience 40
  Keep Your Message Simple 41
  Let the Creative Juices Flow 42
Visual and Verbal Cues 43
  Visual Identity 43
Elements of Good Design... 44
  Proximity 44
  Alignment 45
  Repetition 45
  Contrast 45
  White Space 45
Verbal Identity 46
  One-on-One Communication 47

Part 2: Launching Your Personal Brand   49

5 Brand Identity: Starting with Your Resumé   51

Basic Resumé Design 52
  Get Organized... 53
  What Is Your Goal? 57
  Your Experiences 58
  Branding Marks: Awards and Such 59
Readability 59
Accountability and Accuracy 60
An Introductory Letter 61
  Your Resumé vs. Your Website 62

The Importance of a Portfolio 62
    Choosing Your Portfolio Case........................... 62
    Design Options 62

6 Effective Messaging: Creating Collateral   65

What Do You Really Need? 66
Your Business Card... 66
Your Signature Line 68
Other Marketing Pieces That Accentuate Your
Brand.. 69
    Letterhead 69
    Postcards.. 70
    Brochures... 70
    A Marketing Kit 71
    Bulletin Boards 72
    Billboards... 73

7 Developing Brand Associations   75

Perceptions and Power.. 76
Be a People Person.. 77
Old-School Social Networking.............................. 77
    Building Associations at Work 79
    Join Professional Associations........................... 79
    Attend Professional Conferences....................... 79
    Invite Contacts to Lunch or Breakfast.............. 79
    Become a Board Member................................. 80
    Join the Media 80
    Speak, Publicly.. 80
Brand Associations in the Community 80
    Get Political... 81
    Help Out at Your Church 81
    Coach Your Kid's Team 82
    Show Up for Your Child's Activity................... 82
    Help Out at School 82
    Join Your Neighborhood Group 83
    Volunteer at Charitable Events........................ 83

8 The Total Experience: Living Your Brand   85

Keeping Up Appearances..86
The Importance of Grooming...86
Manners: The Good, the Bad, and the Despicable ...87
   Dine in Style *88*
   The Importance of Saying Thank You.........................*89*
   The Ever-Important Follow-Up *89*
Personal Interactions via Your Body Language 90
   The Handshake...*90*
   Eye Contact *90*
   Standing Stance...*91*
Hosting and Sponsoring Events 91
   Are You a Mingler? *92*
   Rules to Being a Great Host...*92*
   What Does Event Sponsorship Mean? *94*
Your Presence and Availability.......................................95

Part 3: Branding in a Modern World   97

9 Mainstream Media Still Counts   99

A Few Examples 100
Demystifying the Media..100
   What Is Print Media? *101*
What Is Broadcast Media? 103
Working with the Media to Build a Brand.............103
   Publicize Your Achievements *103*
   Become a Source..*104*
   Write a Regular Column *106*
   Write a Book *106*
   Become a Broadcast Star *107*
Hire Outside Help 107

10 Understanding Public Relations   109

What Is Good PR?...110
   Framing Your Message *110*
   The Diffusion Theory of PR...*111*
   Entertaining the Hierarchy of Needs..........................*111*

Tools of the Trade 112
   Media Releases.. 112
   Media Advisories 114
   Letters and Opinion Columns.................... 115
Publicity Photos 116
Media Kits 117
Creating a Public Relations Plan..................... 118

11 Branding Yourself Via the Web **121**
A Personal Branding Story................................ 122
Websites.. 123
   To Get Help, or Not...................................... 123
   Tracking Visitors... 124
Electronic Newsletters 125
E-mail Blasts.. 126
Podcasts 126
Social Networking.. 127
   Facebook and MySpace.................................. 127
   LinkedIn 128
   YouTube 129
   Twitter 129
   Blogs.. 130
   Vlogs 131
   Internet Forums 131
Advantages of Using the Web........................... 131
   Pitfalls of the Online World 132

12 Personal Communication in a New Age **133**
Where Do You Fit In? 134
E-mail 134
Instant Messaging.. 137
Cell Phone Calls... 138
Text Messaging 138
Facebook's Wall Messaging and More 140
The Blogosphere 140
The Wiki 142
To Skype, or Not?... 143
Web Conferencing 143

13 Should You Buy the Mad Ad, Men?   **145**

Why Should You Advertise? 146
When Should You Advertise Your Personal
   Brand? 146
Types of Advertising 148
   Broadcast *148*
   Webcasts *149*
   Websites and Blogs *150*
   Newspapers and Magazines *151*
   The Telephone Book *152*
   Direct Mail *152*
   Personal Letter *153*
   Endorsements and Sponsorships *153*
   Buttons and Bumper Stickers *153*
   Posters *154*
   T-shirts and Other Apparel *154*
   Airplane Banners, Billboards, and More *154*
Devising an Advertising Plan 155

14 Guerrilla Tactics in a Noisy World   **157**

What Is Guerrilla Marketing? 158
A Few Definitions 158
Building a Guerrilla Marketing Campaign 159
   Do Your Research *160*
   Be Creative *161*
   Don't Stop Marketing After the Launch *161*
Building Partnerships 162
Word of Mouth 162
A Few Examples 163
   Living the 1960s *163*
   Yo-Yo Mama *163*
   T-Shirt Exposure *164*
   Million-Dollar Bra *164*
   Derrie-Air *164*
   Biking in Place *164*
   Taking It to the Streets *165*
   Pop-up Businesses *165*
   Staging Events *165*

Guerrilla Marketing and the Law............................ 165
A Guerrilla Marketing Campaign Gone Awry......... 166
Another Tactic Gone Bad 167

Part 4:   Brand Extension and Evolution   169

15 If You Brand It, They Will Come   171

What Is Brand Extension? 172
Ivory Soap 172
Clorox 172
Extending a Personal Brand................................... 172
Jimmy Buffett 173
Ralph and Terry Kovel.. 173
Celebrity Chefs... 173
Paula Deen... 174
Emeril.. 174
Starting Points for Extending Your Personal
Brand... 175
Head to the Classroom 176
Develop Patents, Websites, and Stores....................... 176
Cult Brands... 177
Think Twice Before Extending Your Brand............. 177
More Things to Consider... 178
Brand Measurement 178
What If Your Brand Gets Huge?............................ 179

16 Lessons from Megabrand Personalities   181

Master the Basic Skills 182
Tiger Woods... 182
Rachael Ray... 183
Stay Relevant 183
Madonna.. 183
John McCain.. 184
Big Risks May Pay Off... 185
President Barack Obama... 185
Donald Trump... 186
Have a Passion for Success 186
Ralph Lauren 187
Ellen DeGeneres.. 187

17 Global Responsibility   189

What Is Branding in a Global World? 190
   Live Abroad.. 191
   Study Overseas 192
   International Internships....................................... 192
What Makes a Global Hit? 192
   The Next Level.. 194
Brand Protection 195
Avoiding the Language Barrier 195
Careful with Clichés... 196
Mixed Messages or Worse 197

18 The Smoke and Fog of Branding   199

Setting the Stage 200
Increasing Skepticism... 200
Uphold Your Reputation.. 202
Don't Be Seduced by the Internet 202
   The Story of Jayson Blair....................................... 203
Creating Your Own Anecdote................................. 204
Today's Hyper-Competition 204

19 Being Your Own Brand Barista   207

What Is a Brand Manager? 208
What Is Your Online Brand Image? 208
   How to Fix Your Online Brand Image 208
   Protecting Your Facebook Info.............................. 209
Keeping It Fresh... 210
The Mic Is Never Off... 210
Be Careful with E-mail 211
Brand Management and Your Boss.......................... 212
Managing Your Tone.. 212
Working While Not at Work 213
Managing Your Brand During Dry Spells................ 213
Don't Get Stuck 214
Building a Reservoir 214
Handling Failure and Coming Clean....................... 215
Revitalizing Your Brand 215

20 Branding in the Future **219**

Remaining Flexible in a Changing Economy 220
*Adjusting Your Personal Brand in an Economic
Crisis*.. 220
Growing Categories for Brands 221
Ingenuity Valued: The Creative Class 223
Creativity in Action 224
Life Is Indeed Good 224
Play Goes Big 224
Tap Water for $1 225
Your Long-Term Brand Sustainability 225
Underlying Branding Themes 226
Personal Brand Evolution 227

Appendixes

   A Glossary **229**

   B Resources **235**

     Index **239**

Introduction

Do you have a personal brand? If not, you better get one.

Big companies, such as Coca-Cola and Starbucks, place great importance on creating and promoting their brands, and they know how to make billions of dollars by managing them. You can emulate their success on a smaller scale by developing your own brand as your most important asset.

Your brand is all about creating an emotional bond with a target audience. To create an authentic, effective brand, you need to be honest with yourself about who you are, the skills you have, and what you want to accomplish.

We know a guy with a big personal brand. Gordon Gee is the president of Ohio State University, one of the largest public universities in the country. He has a unique personal style, which involves his trademark bowtie.

The bowtie has gotten him a lot of media attention. But to say that Gordon Gee's brand revolves around his sartorial choices is missing the point. The focus of his personal brand is his passion for higher education. He projects this passion through his charismatic personality and his ability to poke fun at himself. Of course, the bowtie doesn't hurt. And neither do his strong leadership and administrative skills. That full package—Gee's personal brand—has made him a highly respected and sought-after university president. And he earns more than a million dollars a year doing it.

So who needs a personal brand? Anyone who wants to have a successful professional life. In this era of high unemployment, nonstop global communication, and social networking websites, your personal brand is already being shaped, with or without your input.

The Complete Idiot's Guide to Branding Yourself will help you develop your own brand to meet the challenges of this fast-paced, complicated, evolving world and help you stand out from your competition.

Developing a personal brand is valuable to anyone on the verge of a career transition: graduating college students searching for that elusive first job, mid-career professionals looking to change tracks, parents trying to reenter the workplace after raising a family, executives who have suddenly lost their jobs through layoffs and outsourcing, and retirees still wanting to capitalize on their skills.

Brands have the power to change people's lives. They can shape the world. But personal branding is also about how we lead our lives, the contributions we make to our communities, and how we want to improve the places in which we live and work.

How to Use This Book

The *Complete Idiot's Guide to Branding Yourself* is divided into four parts.

In **Part 1, "What Is Branding?,"** you will learn how to develop your own branding story based on your personal and professional goals. You will learn how to assess your brand and how to present your personal elevator pitch. An effective brand is only as good as your ability to communicate its message to others, and the final chapter in this part helps you stand out from the crowd by honing your communication skills.

Part 2, "Launching Your Personal Brand," will help you take the brand you developed in Part 1 and begin projecting it into the world. You will learn how your resumé, portfolio, headshot, and other marketing collateral reflects your brand identity. In addition, you will learn how to effectively and professionally communicate your personal brand via social networks, associations, and partnerships.

Part 3, "Branding in a Modern World," teaches you how to harness the media monster to help promote your brand. You will learn about the various opportunities for promoting your brand through various media channels. These techniques include serving as a media resource for reporters; distributing effective public relations materials; communicating with the world via social networking sites, blogs, and podcasts; and advertising in traditional and new media.

In **Part 4, "Brand Extension and Evolution,"** you will learn you can extend your brand and when you should consider doing so. In addition, you will be introduced to several mega-brand personalities who have made huge successes of their personal brands.

With a big brand comes big responsibility. This part tackles the sticky issue of globalization by offering suggestions for managing a brand in an increasingly global economy. And the final chapter in this section turns toward the future: where does personal branding go from here?

Extras

We give you even more information in the following sidebars, which are scattered throughout the book.

Real World Brands
Read these boxes to find examples of people and companies that have established successful brands.

Warning
Keep your eye out for these red flags when developing and promoting your personal brand.

Tips
Here we offer additional advice on branding yourself.

def•i•ni•tion
Look to these boxes for clear, concise explanations of branding terms.

Acknowledgments

Many people were involved in the making of this book.

We especially want to thank our editor, Michelle Wells, who had the concept for this project long before we walked into the picture.

While working on this book, we relied heavily on our children for advice. Justin Paprocki, a journalist for the *Island Packet* of Hilton Head, South Carolina, has been on the leading edge of Internet usage. His overall knowledge of today's communication techniques, from etiquette to history, was illuminating. And we also appreciated his tips for our chapter on resumés.

Ana Paprocki, who graduates from Boston University in 2009, held our hand as we learned more about social networking and Web 2.0. Because of her wisdom and online skills, she has made sure that we'll never embarrass ourselves via the electronic world.

We need to thank our intern Alex Hurst, a senior at Denison University, who provided research, guidance, and proofreading expertise. More thanks go to our students at Otterbein College, who also gave us feedback regarding their own communication experiences as they built their young brands.

We appreciate the friends who contributed anecdotes and advice, as well as asking provocative questions. And to those who unknowingly made their way into the book—based on various conversations, observations, and experiences through years—we also extend our thanks.

It is impossible to name everyone who has contributed to our careers and served as mentors as we've built our own personal brands. Please know that we are grateful for your help.

Trademarks

All terms mentioned in this book that are known to be or are suspected of being trademarks or service marks have been appropriately capitalized. Alpha Books and Penguin Group (USA) Inc. cannot attest to the accuracy of this information. Use of a term in this book should not be regarded as affecting the validity of any trademark or service mark.

What Is Branding?

Part 1 provides the building blocks for understanding how branding can help you achieve success in your personal and professional life. You will learn what branding is all about and how to create and execute a branding plan. You will learn about the language of branding, what branding is not, and why your personal brand matters so much.

One of the primary goals of Part 1 is to help you write your own branding story. This story will help you determine your goals for the future and how your brand relates to those goals. In addition, you will receive tips about how to reach your target audience and how to get your message heard.

Personal Branding Defined

In This Chapter

♦ Using a brand to stand out from the crowd

♦ Figuring out who you are

♦ Getting familiar with the terminology

♦ Maintaining your personal brand

Branding has been a business buzzword for many years. A brand, though, is more than a snazzy name and logo. It's the core of what a business stands for. It's about generating a positive emotional response in your customers. It's about making people want to buy your goods and services rather than those of your competitors. Companies that have strong brands include IBM, Disney, and FedEx.

A brand stands for something. For instance, people associate Target with stylish products at lower prices. Starbucks' brand is about more than just coffee—it represents a way of life. Victoria's Secret's brand is all about playful sexiness.

You, too, can have a brand. There are more opportunities to build your own brand today than at any other time in history, thanks in large part to the ability to communicate instantaneously through the Internet. But just because opportunities for branding abound, that doesn't mean it's easy to create a strong personal brand. First, you have to distinguish yourself from "the clutter" of everyone else trying to get their own recognition. Creating a personal brand is all about connecting with people to establish who you are and what you can do. It's about telling your own story.

Keep in mind that personal branding is not just about building a bigger audience on the web using social networking tools. It's also about old-fashioned personal interactions—a firm handshake, a thoughtful thank-you note, and following through on commitments. Branding is also about understanding the mainstream media and learning the basic tools of good public relations.

It's time to start promoting Brand You.

Personal Branding Defined

A personal brand is an authentic depiction of who you are, what skills you have developed, and what value you can bring to your work. The ultimate result of building a personal brand is that people—bosses, clients, prospective employers—have a positive emotional response when they hear or read your name. Your brand helps you to get noticed, to stand out.

The good news is that you already have a personal brand. It's your reputation. It's the way people think of you. However, to make the most of your brand, you need to develop it and manage it.

Who Needs a Personal Brand?

Whether you are just getting started in your career or have been working for several years, you can benefit from developing your personal brand. A student graduating from college needs to make a strong impression so he can land that first job. A mid-career manager needs to impress the new boss after the company has been sold. The executive whose job has been cut needs to showcase her unique skills to land another top position. The stay-at-home mom ready to re-enter the job market needs to persuade her prospective employer that her experience brings value to the workplace. The retiree needs to figure out how to transition into a new career.

def•i•ni•tion

Brand position is how companies distinguish themselves from their competition. In personal branding, this is how you make yourself stand out, say, from other job candidates.

Figuring Out Your Brand

So what is unique about you? How do you want people to respond when they hear your name? What is compelling about your ideas? What makes you stand out?

If you're a journalist, you want to be seen as fair, accurate, lively, and informative. You earn that reputation by being consistent. People will begin to trust your writing. Your byline will become a brand.

For instance, we are regular readers of *Newsweek*, and any time there is an article by Fareed Zakaria, Ray always reads it. Zakaria has established a brand for himself as an authority on international affairs. He makes complex topics understandable, provides interesting insights, and chooses lively topics. Ray has enjoyed Zakaria's work so much he bought one of the journalist's books.

Warning

Think hamming it up for the camera or video recorder is fun? Be careful. Thanks to YouTube, it's possible for millions of people all over the world to witness you doing something offensive, embarrassing, or just plain stupid. Over and over and over and over again. That's not good, unless you want people to think that your best quality is the ability to stumble around drunk wearing a sombrero while singing an off-key rendition of "Thriller."

And during the presidential campaign in 2008, we tuned in to CNN to listen to the commentary by David Gergen, the former aide to four presidents, ex-editor of *U.S. News and World Report,* and current director of Harvard University's Center for Public Leadership. He stood out among the screaming-head panelists for his reasoned, calm, and thoughtful analysis of presidential politics.

Your personal brand must be based on an honest assessment of your skills and talents. How do you get someone to have a strong positive emotional response to you? What do people expect when they deal with you?

You build trust by being consistent. You become consistent by being disciplined. Your discipline is fueled by your integrity, your passion, and your desire to stay abreast of all new developments in your chosen field.

def•i•ni•tion

Brand management is about maintaining your brand. Is your brand consistent across everything you do, from your business card to your message on the answering machine to your stationary to your personal presentation? Do you keep your brand current?

What Branding Is Not

Branding may sound like just another way to package and market yourself. It may even seem a bit manufactured and inauthentic. But branding is not about tricking people into buying your services or pretending to be someone you are not.

It's about clearly establishing who you are, what you are good at, or even what you like to do, so you can stand above your competition.

Real World Brands

The last time the Chicago Cubs baseball team won a World Series was in 1908. Despite many losing seasons and heartbreaking losses in important games, fans flock to watch the team play—and millions more view the games on television. What gives these loveable losers such a winning brand? A combination of a rich history, colorful characters, and a charming ballpark (Wrigley Field) has contributed to the Cubs' popularity.

Research has shown that once people, particularly older people, get an impression of a brand, the impression tends to stick. If you have a brand that triggers a negative emotional response, it will be difficult to alter it.

Celebrity Brands

Here are some of the megastars who have built brands for themselves:

- ◆ Oprah Winfrey
- ◆ Michael Jordan
- ◆ Martha Stewart
- ◆ Muhammad Ali
- ◆ Paris Hilton
- ◆ Madonna
- ◆ Tiger Woods
- ◆ Donald Trump

Real World Brands
Ad man Dan Wieden of Portland, Oregon, is credited with creating the famous marketing slogan "Just Do It." It was 1988 and Nike was competing against its rival Reebok in the athletic shoe market. The slogan, combined with a strong product and a memorable campaign featuring such superstars as Bo Jackson and Michael Jordan, turned the company into the world's dominant sporting goods brand.

Each of these people has carved out a strong reputation—albeit some more positive than others. When you hear the name Oprah Winfrey, you think of the media magnate, perhaps the world's most influential woman. When you hear Michael Jordan's name, you think of the greatest basketball player who ever lived. When you hear Paris Hilton, well, you think of someone who is famous for just being famous (as well as for a host of bad behaviors).

Roger Clemens, the great baseball pitcher, was a highly respected brand for several years. And then he got tangled up with the scandal involving performance-enhancing drugs and his brand has been forever changed, perhaps even preventing him from making the Hall of Fame.

One of the most unlikely examples of a successful personal brand is Orville Redenbacher. He looked like a cartoon figure (skinny, big glasses, bow tie) and he was in the very uncool business of selling popcorn. He believed passionately in the quality of this popcorn, however, and became the spokesperson for his company. People embraced him because he was unusual, authentic, and consistent. His popcorn became a big seller.

Brand Loyalty

Our family has had good luck with Toyota vehicles. Ray has owned a 1997 Paseo convertible for close to a decade. It has gone more than 200,000 miles, but it still runs great. Sherry owns a Solara convertible. It, too, has been highly reliable. Because of our positive experiences with these vehicles, we associate the Toyota brand with dependable, safe, and stylish automobiles that get good gas mileage.

At some point, we will be in the market for a new car. We will more than likely skip the hours of research in *Consumer Reports* and head straight to the Toyota dealership. Why? Those two magic words: consistency and trustworthiness. That's brand loyalty.

Speaking of *Consumer Reports*, that's another trusted brand. It's a source of independent, thorough, and objective research. People spend thousands of dollars based solely on its recommendation. That's a hard brand to beat. Yet, if there was ever any controversy surrounding the ratings, any hint the publication was not independent or unbiased, the brand would suffer.

Your goal should be to build that same kind of loyalty into your brand.

def•i•ni•tion

Brand equity is the value your brand holds. It's hard to quantify, but it's the reason a client is willing to pay for your services even if they are higher than your competitors'. It's because he knows you will deliver high quality time and time again.

How to Assess Yourself

Ask tough questions: What are my weaknesses? What personal characteristics irritate people? How do I compare to other people with similar skill sets and experience?

You might want to follow the model established by businesses trying to build their brands: market surveys. They spend a lot of money to find out what people like and dislike about their products. Of course, you're not going to employ a sophisticated marketing team to survey people about your personal brand. But you can take a similar approach: ask your colleagues, clients, friends, and family members for their thoughts. Find out what they think are your strengths and weaknesses.

What is your niche? What is the market and how can you fill it?

You should be able to say, "Here's what I stand for." Then use that brand to understand how to build a career. Business people who build brands believe in what they are creating. You have to believe in yourself.

Be an Expert

It's easier to build a personal brand if you can become an expert in your field. Take the case of two savvy financial planners. Both have a broad-based knowledge about investment planning, but one of them also specializes in helping wealthier clients invest in oil exploration. Her expertise and contacts in this field help set her apart.

You want to become a go-to, top-of-the-mind person—whether it's in your company or while building your own one-person shop. You want people to say, "Oh, yeah, if it involves [area of expertise], then we need to get [fill in your name]."

Managing Your Brand

Once you establish your brand, it's time to sit back and relax, right? Wrong. The worst thing you can do is work hard to establish a brand and then let it languish without proper care and feeding. Your brand will become tarnished if it's not tended to regularly.

Make sure you evaluate all the elements of your brand periodically. Are your business cards current? If you have a blog, is it up-to-date? Are you staying on top of the trends in your field?

Tips

Les Wexner, the CEO and founder of Limited Brands, which is the parent company of such famous brands as Victoria's Secret and Bath & Body Works, has reinvented himself and his business throughout a career that now spans more than 40 years. One of his professors at Ohio State University once told him that he should get in the habit of changing—rearrange his desk routinely, for instance. The idea was to incorporate change (and respond to it) as part of his life so he could become flexible in a business world that doesn't stand still.

And realize that you project your brand through your appearance, your manner, your messages, and the materials you use to spread those messages. Managing your brand is not a part-time job.

Without consistent maintenance, your brand begins to look sloppy and outdated. And those aren't exactly the characteristics you want to be associated with.

The Least You Need to Know

- Building a personal brand requires self-examination.
- Get ready to ask yourself tough questions about who you are and about your strengths and weaknesses.
- The keys to brand building are consistency and trustworthiness.
- It's good to be modest … to a point. It's okay to publicize your achievements.
- Everything you do reflects on your brand.

2

Writing Your Own Branding Story

In This Chapter

- ◆ Creating an authentic brand
- ◆ Branding is about perception and reputation
- ◆ Writing a personal branding statement
- ◆ Positioning yourself in the competitive career marketplace

We get branded all the time without even trying. Our family, friends, colleagues, and even people who don't know us, such as politicians and marketers, decide who we are and what we stand for based on how we look, what we do and say, and the purchases we make. And although we can't completely control what people think of us, we can influence their perceptions. This is what branding is all about.

This chapter explains why it is important to establish a personal brand. You will learn about brand authenticity, and you will gain the necessary tools to write your own branding story.

Brand Authenticity

An authentic brand is an honest brand. It makes true claims about its products, services, or whatever it represents. Similarly, an authentic personal brand is an honest portrayal of you, your talents, and your skills.

> **Warning**
>
> Build an authentic personal brand based on your core values. If you don't, you may be surprised at what an employer or client can find out about you during an Internet search by using Google or Yahoo!. One small business owner thought he knew everything about his partner. But then he discovered through an online search of court documents that several years ago his partner had filed for bankruptcy when he owned another business. The news shook the trust established between the two men.

For instance, many companies have been accused of brand inauthenticity in their claims to be environmentally friendly. Even though they branded themselves as "green," in reality they were not following earth-friendly and sustainable practices. They were using the green theme as a marketing tool, but they were greenwashing, or faking their actual concern for the environment.

Starbucks is a good example of a company that created great brand authenticity when it first started. For many years, the Seattle-based company thrived with its branding story about being a warm, local, wholesome coffee bar that served up a cup of fresh-brewed coffee with a big grin from the barista. The corporation stressed environmental sustainability and local community. But as the company grew from its Seattle base to more than 13,000 stores around the world, the mega-brand began losing some of its small shop authenticity. By mid-2008, with the economy in a recession, people became focused more on cost savings than on a $4 cup of coffee. Starbucks began closing stores. Its brand authenticity had been watered down. Starbucks no longer fit the distinctive brand image that it had built.

Brand authenticity is even more important when it comes to your personal brand. For example, we know a small business owner who consults with other families to help them become more environmentally conscious. It is imperative to her personal brand that, at home and at her office, she has a well-organized recycling setup.

No matter what your profession, authenticity is key. If you're a physician, you'll want to be sure that your record with the state licensure agency is squeaky clean. If you're a contractor, you'll want to know the business of building inside and out, and have a long list of clients who will vouch for you.

Know Yourself

Psychologists say that being authentic, or true to yourself, will make you a happier, more content person. To be authentic as a person, you must recognize your true self. You should be aware of your own tastes, emotions, and abilities. You should understand yourself enough to know what type of work you enjoy and what type of work you are good at.

Being authentic also means that you sometimes may be criticized or rejected because you express your own values and needs. Your opinions and values will not always be the same as those of your friends and even your family. To be authentic means that you are open and honest about your true feelings and that you understand yourself.

Tips

Some Eastern religions believe that people more often do the right things when they are being authentic to their core values. Psychologists have suggested that being authentic may make you less likely to get addicted to drugs, alcohol, and other substances.

Get Real for Your Personal Brand

As you continue to consider your authentic self, begin to think about your personal brand. Is your brand authentic to the core of your personal values? Do you live your life aligned with morals that you believe are good and true? Do you treat people with dignity and respect? Being authentic also means that you accept your own personal faults and failings. You know what you excel at, and you know your weaknesses.

If you are creating an authentic brand, you must be aware that anything you do in private life can also affect your public life. Your private actions—whether being arrested for drunk driving, treating clerks or customer service personnel poorly, or failing to keep commitments—can become very public very quickly.

If you are hanging out with employees or with co-workers, whatever you say and do in that group of people will reflect on your personal brand.

Building Your Brand Is Work

It is easy to talk about being true to yourself and to believe that you are doing good things. In fact, it is far easier to talk about these things than it is to put your brand into action.

For example, a lot of people think they would like to open a restaurant. It may be a small coffee shop, a specialty ice cream parlor, or a full-serve establishment. These potential owners get excited talking about the concept for the restaurant, its location, and what they would serve. But in actuality, the real work begins when the doors open and customers are clamoring for service, staff members are still being trained, and the owners are exhausted as they work all hours of the day and night to try to make their dreams come true. Many new restaurants last barely a year before their doors close, their owners exhausted and, more often than not, broke.

Authentic brand action, whether you're interested in becoming a restaurateur, a serious writer, or a real estate broker, means that you have established a deep knowledge of that field and you are prepared for the rigors of entering it. Over time you develop a trustworthy and dependable brand to which your audience will respond.

Why Write Your Branding Story Now?

To position yourself in the marketplace, it's important that you consider your personal branding story. Some of the most affluent and influential people of our time started out by examining their short- and long-term goals and creating a story, with them in the starring role, achieving those goals.

Your branding story doesn't have to be lengthy or complex. Think about the branding story of a computer repairman who we know. If one of our computers fails to boot up in the morning, we can give him a call and he shows up in an hour or two. More often than not, the computer will start working by nightfall of the same day. This man has a terrific branding story.

He's authentic. He loves technology and is passionate about discussing it with his clients. He seems to know everything that could possibly be wrong with a computer. He recommends the most cost-efficient method of dealing with a problem. He always returns phone calls and he's more than willing to give advice if you're searching for a new computer. If he feels that his advice was inadequate, the next time you call him he's likely to give you a discount off his already reasonable hourly rate. If he doesn't know something, he's willing to say so. He's a down-to-earth person who works from his home and enjoys a simple life. And he's happy being a freelance consultant who has no desire to grow a bigger business. He's a man who knows his strengths, his weaknesses, and his goals in life.

Now consider the branding story of a comedian you may know: Ellen DeGeneres. Her biggest asset is being funny. DeGeneres has very little college education, but she knew that one day she wanted to make a living by making people laugh. She had a goal. She did a lot of stand-up comedy at small clubs across the country early in her career and became Showtime's Funniest Person in America in 1982. Even though she makes telling jokes look easy, she worked hard and got better at her craft through the years. By the mid-1990s she had her own television sit-com. But after the lead character came out as being gay—about the same time that DeGeneres announced that *she* was gay—the sit-com failed.

DeGeneres went back to her roots and started doing stand-up acts again. As a comedian in California, she was dependable and available. She was willing to show up at luncheons and do television specials. Without fail, she continued to be funny. She hosted *Saturday Night Live* and appeared on numerous talk shows. In 2003 she launched her own daytime talk show called *The Ellen DeGeneres Show*, which has been a raging success and won several daytime Emmy Awards. Just like our computer guy, Ellen DeGeneres is a person who knows her strengths, her weaknesses, and her goals in life.

Tips

You can begin considering your branding story during idle moments while driving, taking a shower, or during commercials of a baseball game you're watching on television. Or make an appointment with yourself at the local coffee shop and take along your notebook for company. It's okay to have a Branding Yourself meeting on your weekly schedule. It doesn't take long to jot down a few key points about where you're headed in the future.

It's About Your Reputation

Branding is all about reputation. Think about some of the biggest personal brands of our time: Oprah Winfrey, Donald Trump, Martha Stewart, and Tiger Woods. Even though their personal brands are hugely divergent, these four people all started very early in their lives thinking about their futures and their future career goals.

Real World Brands

To preserve her reputation during and after she served time in prison, Martha Stewart took the advice of brand-building guru Charles Koppelman. He helped her transition the leadership of her company to other people when it became apparent that she would go to prison. Koppelman helped Stewart preserve her big personal brand, so that it was still intact and worth a lot of money when she was released. He advised her to write a book about business, called *The Martha Rules,* and he encouraged her to establish a channel on the Sirius station. Koppelman was Stewart's right-hand man on *The Apprentice: Martha Stewart,* which appeared upon her release from prison. Koppelman has also advised Steve Madden, the rapper Vanilla Ice, and Michael Jackson.

Oprah Winfrey was raised by her poor grandmother and faced many challenges early in life, but she never gave up the chance to read and learn. Donald Trump continually challenged conventional wisdom to become one of the most successful developers in the world. Martha Stewart was a housewife who liked to cook and entertain before she started her catering business, which quickly grew to include planning events for some of the most notable people in her community. Tiger Woods started to golf as a child, and with his father's strong encouragement grew into the greatest golfer of today.

All of these people worked tirelessly to pursue their passion. They were dependable and persistent, and rarely, if ever, failed to uphold their brand. Each established a reputation of excellence, dependability, and consistency. They have built authentic brands based on their core values. Some of them have reputations for being nice, others have reputations for being harsh businessmen and women. Nonetheless, their reputations are a big part of their personal brands.

Branding is important to people of all ages who are looking to build a good reputation within their chosen field. Branding yourself will help focus and perpetuate the good things that you want to achieve in your life.

Ask Yourself Some Questions

To begin the process of writing your personal branding story, ask yourself the following questions:

What am I known for? (List three items.)

What do I want to be known for five years from today? (List three items.)

What do I want people to say about me at my retirement party? (List five items.)

What new and updated terms have I learned in the last year? (List as many as possible.)

What new skill do I plan to learn within the next year so that my personal brand is up-to-date? (List one item.)

Do I look, act, and dress in a way that reflects my personal brand? (Answer yes or no to all three parts of this question.)

Do my actions reflect the brand I want to present?

How many upcoming meetings do I have on my calendar with people who will enhance my professional abilities?

Think about your personality, your skills, your knowledge, and how you want to position yourself as a professional.

Create a Personal Branding Statement

The answers to the above questions will provide you with clues and notes for your branding story. To begin writing your personal branding story, take on the role of being your own personal *brand manager*. First, create a definition of yourself. What can you say about yourself in a sentence or two? Here are some examples:

"Hi, I'm Ralph, and I'm the author of three books about business branding."

"My name is Jane Smith and I am a dermatologist who specializes in microderm abrasion."

"Hello, I'm Todd Smith and I am a residential contractor."

"Hi, I'm JD and I just graduated from NYU with a degree in theater. Last summer I interned at the Shakespeare Theater Company in Washington."

"I'm Pamela Jones and I own a graphic design business."

"Hi, I'm Leroy. I'm an attorney who specializes in bankruptcy law."

"Hello, my name is Dan. I'm a retired Navy captain and I teach history at the local high school. I'm campaigning to be elected as a representative in the state legislature."

"Hi, I'm Elmo. I'm the only plumber in town."

def•i•ni•tion

A **brand manager** is a person or a group of people who controls the brand of a company or a nonprofit entity. A brand manager protects the brand's image by overseeing the use of its logo and other brand identifiers. When you're branding yourself, keep in mind that you are your own brand manager who makes sure that your reputation goes unsullied.

Write a brief sentence that will serve as your personal branding statement. This is an introduction to your branding story.

_____

_____

_____

_____

Focus on your strengths.

Elaborate

Once you have your personal branding statement, you can extend it into a full story by reflecting on key characteristics about your personal brand:

- Are you technologically savvy?

- Do you have special technical skills such as designing programs or websites?

- Have you been a team player since your preschool years?

- Do you have the ability to solve challenges with the keen savvy of an engineer?

- Do you approach a problem with strategic, creative, out-of-the-box thinking?

- Are you a great team manager?

- Are you a clear communicator with impeccable writing skills?

- What else makes you stand apart?

Answering these questions will help you as you write your personal branding story.

Ask for Input from Others

Once you have had some time to reflect on your personal attributes, ask others for input. Friends, family members, and colleagues will have unique insights about you, your skills, and your personality. Some questions to ask:

- What am I good at?

- What do you think I like to do?

- Am I good at what I like to do?

- Do I have skills that others in my field do not have?

- Are there other ways that I stand out from the crowd?

By asking others these questions, you might discover areas of expertise that you took for granted that others highly value.

> **Tips**
>
> If you are married or in a long-term relationship, how will your personal brand affect your partner? It is important that a partner understands and is supportive of your self-branding efforts, as that person may be affected by your personal brand building.

It's a good reality check to discuss this journey into branding yourself with other people who know you well and who will share their honest thoughts—both positive and negative—with you. Building a good, solid personal brand requires grassroots input. That's why so many companies develop focus groups and marketing surveys to test and discuss a new product before they consider releasing it.

Writing Your Branding Story

Finally, with input from others and a thorough evaluation of your own skills and professional goals, you can write the core story about your personal brand. Take some time to scratch out or type 200 to 500 words that uniquely describe your talents and skills. In the end, your all-encompassing branding story will help determine the branding niche that you will adopt.

Here's JD's completed branding story:

> Hi, I'm JD and I just graduated from NYU with a degree in theater. Last summer I interned at the Shakespeare Theater Company in Washington. I'm a versatile actor and comedian who

would like to eventually live in New York. But, to get started I would be willing to travel around the country with a theater group that performs at high schools and colleges. My passion is improv, but I understand that there are very few jobs in that field. If I had the opportunity, I would like to act on *Saturday Night Live* or work for *Second City in Chicago*. Eventually, I'd like to have my own television talk show and be like Jon Stewart. My acting skills are superb, although my social presentation skills may need a little work. I'm somewhat shy around people that I don't know, unless I'm acting on a stage somewhere. I have great computer skills, but I have no desire to work at a computer all day long. Some people tell me that I should be an animator, but it's not my passion. My goal is not to make a lot of money, but to fulfill my dream of being famous one day.

Here's the branding story of Pamela Jones, the graphic design business owner.

I'm Pamela Jones and I own a graphic design business. Years ago, I received my graphic design training at the Savannah College of Art and Design. After designing catalogs for a major retailer, I wanted to branch out on my own so that I could use my creative skills. I opened a graphic design studio in an old brick building on Fourth Street and had a lot of fun decorating its offices in vibrant, bold colors and eclectic furniture and artwork. I have a few clients to start with, such as the local college and two local restaurants. But, my goal is to have a staff of four or five graphic designers who work for me so that we can help small businesses create their own brands. I guess I'm pretty good at design work, because I've won about five different national awards for small magazines that I've designed for the college. I like working with younger design-ers and teaching them some of the tricks that I've learned through the years. And, I like surprising my clients with designs that they never could have imagined. Some people think that graphic design is a business that you could just do in your free time, but that's not true. I work many long hours at my studio and I always hit deadlines. My clients are very important to me and I try to make them feel that way. I'm really environmentally conscious. When I was remodeling my building, I made sure that everything from the paint to the glue used for the carpet was environmentally safe. Environmental sustainability is very important to me on a personal level.

Summarizing Your Branding Story into an Elevator Pitch

Take some more time to filter out the trivial thoughts regarding your branding story and boil it down to a short verbal explanation about who you are and what you do. This is called an *elevator pitch*. An elevator pitch is different from your branding story because it's shorter and sums up your abilities. Sometimes your elevator pitch is very similar to your initial branding statement. But, more often, you have overlooked a few things when writing your branding statement that have been revealed while you write your entire branding story. You may be surprised at the number of opportunities you have to present the elevator pitch about your brand.

def•i•ni•tion

An **elevator pitch** is a brief description—one that you can get out in the time it takes while taking a short elevator ride. An elevator pitch should be less than 100 words.

Below is JD's elevator pitch, which he may give to a theater director he meets at a party one evening. Notice how it's different from his initial branding statement:

> Hi, I'm JD and I just graduated from NYU with a degree in theater. Last summer I interned at the Shakespeare Theater Company in Washington, but my real passion is improv and comedy. I'd love to work for *Saturday Night Live* and become the next Jimmy Fallon with my own talk show.

Now check out Pamela's elevator pitch:

> Hi, my name is Pamela Jones and I own the graphic design business in that funky brick building on Fourth Street. I used to design catalogs for The Red Barn but now I like to do branding work for local businesses that want to promote their environmental consciousness.

Balancing Your Brand

A brand positioning manager at a large corporation needs to be aware of the other brands around him or her. A brand is built around a unique product that fits into the whole corporate scope.

It is just as important for you, as you build your personal brand, to take a look at the people around you to determine whether you fit a niche. If you're already employed, you'll want to look around at your peers and co-workers to determine how well you fit onto the team. Do you bring skills and advantages that would be lacking if you weren't on the team? Or do you duplicate the skills and advantages of others already on the team? Are you in the process of learning new skills that will make you unique on the team and will accelerate your position upward as an indispensable team member?

Position yourself in your professional world so that you have outstanding attributes that will set you apart. In the end, developing your unique personal brand will lead you down fruitful paths—whether it's within the same company or in an entirely different scenario.

Brand Perception

Brand perception is how people see your brand. Try to make sure that the perception others have of your personal brand is in your best, professional interest. You must always keep in mind the perception that others have of your brand in its many variations, from online sites such as Facebook or MySpace to one-on-one conversation with strangers.

Real World Brands

What started as a social networking website for Harvard students back in 2004 has turned into a big business for Facebook founder Mark Zuckerberg. Now based in Palo Alto, California, the company's value is estimated at $15 billion. Zuckerberg, who was a Harvard sophomore at the time of its development but later dropped out of college, has an estimated worth of $1.5 billion, according to Forbes.

What your audience sees in your Facebook persona, for example, may be far from what you deem as the truth about your personal brand when it comes to establishing a reputable career. How stay-at-home parents present themselves at the coffee shop early in the morning after dropping the kids off at school will be the way they are perceived by the professionals who may be on their way to the office at the same time. Either way, brand perception will mean a lot to your future.

How people perceive your brand is of growing importance in our global economy. With the common ability to communicate around the clock, it is important to consider brand perception as one of the key parts of branding yourself.

Brand Positioning

Once you have a clear idea about your personal branding story, you'll want to consider your brand position. When a large company begins an effort to brand a product, one of the first things that key managers do is to look carefully at brand positioning.

Think about the retailer Abercrombie & Fitch. The position of this brand is geared to teenagers who want to be cool. Teens who are hungry for independence. Back in 1988 when billionaire retailer Leslie Wexner purchased Abercrombie & Fitch, it was merely a store in New York City that focused on outdoor equipment and apparel. Wexner and Abercrombie & Fitch CEO Michael Jeffries repositioned the brand as one for the cool kids—just check the pictures on the walls and the attitude of the sales staff when you have the opportunity to visit an Abercrombie & Fitch store. They tapped into the need for independence that all teens experience, as well as their free-spending attitudes.

Abercrombie & Fitch's brand was focused on a specific target audience: teenagers. Teens liked that. In a 2006 survey, teens named A&F the top brand that was targeted at them. This focus on teenagers became the prototype for other copycat companies that have benefited from the same targeted niche: flip-flop wearing, belly-showing teenagers who seek the ultimate state of coolness.

Your Brand Positioning Statement

Your brand position will probably be quite different from the position that Wexner chose for Abercrombie & Fitch. Nonetheless, keep in mind that brand positioning will have a lot to do with whether you get noticed in your own professional niche. To be clear about your position, use your branding story to help you write one last assignment. This is your personal brand positioning statement.

A brand positioning statement will include information from your branding story or your shorter elevator pitch, but it will also suggest ways that make you distinct in your field of expertise. To prepare to write your brand positioning statement, answer these questions:

- ◆ Name two to three things that make you unique in your field.

- ◆ Can you express these distinctive qualities in simple language that most people will understand? For example, you can say, "I won a national award from the Council for Advancement and Support of Education." Or you can say, "I won a national award for a college publication."

- ◆ Can you back up your distinctions with credible background material, if you are asked to do that?

Once you have sorted through the attributes that make you distinct from others in the field, you can more easily write your brand positioning statement. It should be no longer than 150 words. Here's a brand positioning statement for JD:

> Hi, I'm JD and I just graduated from NYU with a degree in theater. Last summer I was the only college student across the country selected to intern at the Shakespeare Theater Company in Washington. During college I also won "Funniest Guy of the Year" award two years in a row.

Now, check out Pamela's brand positioning story:

> Hi, my name is Pamela Jones and I own a graphic design studio. As a catalog designer for The Red Barn, I won four national design awards. Just last year I won another national award for an environmentally-friendly brochure that I designed for the local college's biology department.

The Least You Need to Know

◆ Start your personal brand with a branding statement.

◆ Your authentic brand depends on your reputation and how people perceive it.

◆ Your personal branding story should focus on your strengths.

◆ The elevator pitch derived from your branding story should be no longer than 100 words.

◆ Your brand positioning statement should include information that distinguishes you from others who have the same target audience.

3

Reaching Your Target Audience

In This Chapter

- ◆ Identifying your target audience
- ◆ Determining the goals of your target audience
- ◆ Keeping your brand relevant by updating your skills
- ◆ Strengthening your knowledge about your chosen field

To further examine the position of your brand, consider your target audience and the goals and perceptions of that target audience.

A target audience includes the people to whom a brand is focused. If you're searching for a job, your target audience involves the people who will make the decision to hire you. If you're starting a business, your target audience will involve your clients or customers.

The audience for your personal brand will include the key managers who hire you because they have decided that you fit into the brand they've developed for their team or company.

If you're a recent college graduate, for example, targeting yourself toward a job as a communication specialist for professional sporting team, your target audience will be the team's general manager, coaching staff, and other staff members who will consider your background, your personality, and your resumé before they decide whether you fit onto their staff.

On the other hand, if you're building your own business, your target audience will be the customers who will purchase your goods or services. Consider the needs of your potential clients and what they wish to achieve by hiring you or buying your product.

Examining the Needs of Your Target Audience

No single product can be everything to everyone. All products and services—whether it's a box of detergent or your massage services—have a strategic relevance in today's world.

In Chapter 2 we asked you what you would like to be known for five years from now. Whether that's working for a Fortune 500 company, owning a small business, or being a recognized writer or television personality, there are certain paths to follow.

Examining your target audience involves everything that you can learn about its members. If you want to be hired as an engineer at a large industrial construction company, you'll want to learn about several of those companies, examine the experience that they're looking for when hiring employees, look at the colleges their employees come from, and find out the expertise they most often seek.

Consider the commitment, hours, and expertise that these companies require of their employees. Read articles about such companies, examine their websites for product and career information, and perhaps even interview some employees who hold jobs similar to the jobs you would like to hold.

The same advice should be followed if you're hoping to establish a small business or a career as a writer, actor, or artist. Examine the audience that you are targeting. Identify the functional skills that will make you valuable in that market. Are your experiences relevant to the target audience that would hire you? Will your target audience perceive your experiences as valuable attributes to their company or profession?

Determining your brand relevance to your target audience—potential employers or customers—consider what that company is looking for and whether your areas of expertise are relevant to their current search. Do you have the technological, intellectual, emotional, and social skills to meet their needs?

Differentiation: Do You Have Functional Advantages?

Having a *functional advantage* means you have something that sets you apart from other professionals in your field. You are professionally superior to others in the same market.

Successful brands fill a niche. Consider, again, the clothing retailer Abercrombie & Fitch. At the time the company was rebranded as a hip store for teenagers and college students, it filled a niche that few—if any—others were considering.

def•i•ni•tion

A **functional advantage** is an attribute that makes a brand stand out among its competitors.

Examine your own experiences to determine whether you have a functional advantage. If you're considering opening a bakery, do you have the functional advantage of a collection of your grandmother's old-fashioned cookie recipes that have been handed down through generations? If you're planning to open an auto repair shop, do you have the functional advantage of skills and passion for rebuilding car engines?

Once you have considered your functional advantage, look around at your peers. If you're an Ivy League graduate, is your functional advantage greater than the advantage that your peers offer? Creating a functional advantage means that you, alone, stand out in the marketplace when a company is looking to hire someone.

Perhaps you are a physician in a small community where there are already a number of other family doctors. How can you distinguish yourself from the crowd? One female doctor we know specializes in serving post-menopausal women. She has taken extra courses and studied about the issues these patients face, and she does an e-mail blast periodically to alert her patients in that age range to new research reported in the field.

If you're a chef, you'll want to distinguish yourself from all the other chefs around. We know one chef who specializes in dishes created with organic, local produce. He spends his Saturday mornings at the farmer's market down the street from the restaurant buying tomatoes and eggs right off the back of a farmer's truck. When he has the opportunity, he promotes himself in the local media focusing on his love of cooking with extremely fresh foods. His functional advantage is working in close proximity to the weekly market and taking full advantage of it.

Plumbers, too, can have functional advantages. Sometimes they're learned at a trade school, or sometimes they come with years of experience. There's a plumber in the town where we live who has developed an expertise for repairing pipes in historic homes. He knows, for example, that if a vintage pipe is needlessly replaced it will probably affect the plumbing throughout the house and lead to an eventual replacement of all pipes. (That's because shaking old pipes while replacing only one will probably harm all of the others involved.) His functional advantage is that he's been working in historic homes for about 30 years and has witnessed nearly every plumbing catastrophe one can imagine.

Depth of Knowledge

Having a depth of knowledge in any chosen field will lead to expertise and boost your personal branding efforts. Acquiring a deep-rooted understanding, not only about a specific job, but also about the industry in which that job is located, will provide additional depth to your branding efforts.

You can acquire this depth of knowledge any number of ways. It may involve accomplishing coursework in a chosen area, collecting career experiences in that area, joining professional organizations, reading professional trade journals, and visiting websites targeted to that field.

Branding experts often take a broad-based look at the field of their focus. They look at the industry today and what may occur in it in the future. Then, they identify areas in which there may be opportunities and they gear up their efforts to fill a specific niche.

Tips

In mid-career, it may be easier to reinvent yourself within the same professional field rather than to rebrand yourself in an entirely new industry. That's because you have already accumulated a broad-based knowledge about your field.

For example, if you are a marketing professional, it's important to not only understand the old-school marketing techniques that involve newspaper and television advertising. It's also imperative to understand how social marketing techniques, such as Facebook, YouTube, podcasts, and Twitter, can play into your marketing plan.

Your approach to branding yourself should be similar. Study the industry, the market, and your own attributes. Then, decide the niche that needs filled and design your brand around that niche. To be able to accomplish this task, you will need a broad depth of knowledge in your chosen field.

Forging an Emotional Bond

You can be the most skilled professional in your industry, but if you are unable to connect emotionally with your target audience, you will very likely fail to create a successful brand for yourself.

The success of Victoria's Secret, also developed by retailing tycoon Leslie Wexner, depended heavily on the fact that the chain established good *emotional resonance*

def•i•ni•tion

Emotional resonance is the connection or bond that a brand has with its target audience.

with its core group of customers—women. Women want to look good and feel sexy in their bras and underwear.

We know an advertising sales rep at a magazine who has great emotional resonance with her clients. She understands their businesses and has empathy for them during difficult economic times. She tries to create advertising opportunities that fit into their budget, even in the worst of times. After more than 20 years in the field, she has a strong emotional bond with her clients.

Real World Brands

Les Wexner, founder of Limited Brands, paid $1 million for a small underwear chain in 1982 from a San Francisco businessman who had founded the company so that men would feel comfortable buying lingerie for their wives or girlfriends. Wexner's ah-ha moment was when he realized that his target audience was female, not male. Women wanted to look and feel sexy.

Emotional resonance is related to very basic human desires. We like the way a product appeals to our senses—they way it looks, smells, sounds, tastes, and feels. (Why else would Abercrombie use its special cologne on all of its clothes?) We buy bed sheets with a higher thread count because they feel good at night. Women of all ages buy Australian-branded Ugg boots because they make their feet feel warm when the weather is cold and the skies are dark.

Establishing emotional resonance for your personal brand won't be quite as complicated as it is for retailers and manufacturers that are attempting to build emotional resonance for a product or service. Still, establishing that emotional resonance can be challenging. After all, you're putting your most prized product—yourself—at risk.

We know a woman who plays tennis five days a week. She also goes to a chiropractor. She chose her chiropractor because she is also a tennis player, and many of her tennis friends also go to her, because they feel that she completely understands their needs based on the activities that they do.

Relating to Your Audience

Your ability to relate to your target market in a professional and personal manner at the same time is important. Keep in mind that before you begin attempting to establish emotional resonance, you should already have examined your functional advantages and built a depth of knowledge regarding the company and industry.

Armed with that deep knowledge—and experience—you will feel more comfortable portraying a more passionate side of your personality during preliminary meetings and interviews. By allowing that passion to reveal itself, you will test your ability to establish personal resonance.

During a self-branding effort, creating an emotional bond may feel much more personal and risky than it does for corporations such as Procter & Gamble as they create a product brand. Yet creating an emotional tie with influential people in your target market—whether that is your boss, your professor, or casual acquaintances who can help you build your brand—will pay off for many years to come. Don't be afraid to show your personality, your knowledge, and your goodwill as you begin the endeavor of establishing a good, emotional resonance with your target audience.

Brand Messaging

As you begin building your authentic personal brand, you will want to determine whether you have correctly identified and addressed the needs of your target audience. Meet and talk with creative individuals who are constantly evaluating their own brands. Consider whether your brand is flexible enough to change with these ever-changing times. Use your intuitive and perceptive instincts to decide when changes are needed.

Evolving Needs in the Marketplace

Reading the help wanted ads, as well as visiting websites such as Craigs-list, Monster, and CareerBuilder, will help you determine how your chosen field is changing today. The media is a good example of an evolving industry. Back in the days when newspapers wanted only writers, various trade publications published dozens of advertisements for reporters. Today, though, with the onset of the myriad opportunities available via the web, newspapers not only want newsroom employees who can write, they also want people who are capable of producing audio and video content that can be posted to the web. Suddenly, newsroom employees have become film and radio producers *in addition* to having good writing skills.

> **Tips**
>
> Rapid advances in technology keep many industries in a constant state of flux. Job titles come and go with every new technological breakthrough. Be sure to research your chosen field so that you know if jobs are available in the niche that you desire.

Be an Expert

The day has passed when being a generalist was in your best interest. Carving out your own areas of expertise will strengthen your brand. Thus, if you are an English major and decide that you want a career as a writer, your area of expertise will depend on what you would like to write. Would you like to be known as someone who writes poems, or as a journalist who reports on corporate business? Would you like to be known as a parenting expert because you write a parenting column for the local newspaper, or would you like to be known as a design expert because you write magazine articles about homes and furniture?

Being an expert means looking closely at the area in which you excel and deciding which niches to fill.

Enhance your reputation of being an expert by positioning yourself as an expert every time the opportunity arises. Enter competitions and win awards in your field. Put announcements in the local newspapers when you get a promotion, change a job, or speak at a large conference. Establishing yourself as an expert takes energy, drive, and passion, but it will pay off for many years to come.

Two Ways to Connect

Any brand relates to its audience in at least two ways—a technical, knowledge-based way and a psychological (or emotional) way. In other words, first, you should establish a knowledge base in the field; second, you need to create an emotional bond. Thus, as you begin to create brand awareness, these are the two paths that you will want to consider. In other words, if you are a journalist you first need to know the facts, then you must be able to communicate those facts in your writing in a way that it elicits interest from your readers. If you are a dentist, of course, you must have the knowledge that comes along with a dental degree. But you should also have a good chair-side manner that makes your patients comfortable when they're in the dental chair. Through our lives we've known some dentists with great story-telling abilities and good senses of humor. Certainly, that skill has helped them build successful practices. To create brand awareness, the goal is to have your target audience understand your core areas of expertise. In other words, your branding story should be one that is familiar among the people in your audience. You should have a knowledge base about your craft that makes you stand apart from the crowd.

For example, to stand out from her competitors, a local Realtor must establish herself as an expert in a particular area, and she must also be able to connect with her clients on an emotional level. Perhaps the Realtor's niche is selling homes to buyers of modest income. She establishes her reputation by finding affordable homes for her clients and also having a solid grasp of the mortgage industry in order to help her clients secure financing for their homes. On an emotional level, that Realtor may be able to establish a bond with his or her clients by putting the clients' needs and desires first.

Create Trust

Reputable brands create trust. Consumers purchase specific types of ice cream, for example, because they know it will deliver the creamy satisfaction that they want. They may buy a certain type of toilet paper because they trust it will be soft. There are many ways that brands instill trust.

As you continue developing your personal brand, create trust with your target audience by being an honest, credible person who does what he says he will do in the time frame specified. There are various ways that you can create trust:

◆ Finish projects on time and prior to deadlines.

◆ Dress and act in a manner that is consistent with your professional brand.

◆ Arrive promptly for meetings and regularly attend them.

◆ Prove that your skills are exceptional by consistently doing the best work possible.

◆ Offer advice and expertise in areas that your employers or clients may not be savvy to. For example, if you're adept at using Facebook, YouTube, and other social networking sites, you may have advice to offer that no one else in the office can contribute.

◆ Respect others—whether or not they are your superiors—during meetings and conversations.

In today's challenging economy, earning the trust of your employers and clients is an important part of developing your own brand. With mergers and acquisitions occurring among corporations every day, new corporate employers, for example, will want to trust that you will get the job done despite the turmoil that a corporate buyout almost always brings with it. A transition from one corporate owner to the next often instills a sense of distrust among employees. If you can be the employee that the new corporate owners trust will get the job done, you are on your way to developing a trustworthy brand with the new company.

Recent college graduates and those new to the job market will want to begin establishing a personal brand that evolves around being credible and trustworthy. Employers will want to trust that you will show up for work each day, that you will have an upbeat and can-do attitude no matter how trivial the job may be, and that you will bring knowledge-based skills that others in the office may not have. No matter what your age and pedigree, establishing trust for your personal brand can begin the minute you accept your first assignment.

The Least You Need to Know

- Distinguish yourself from your peers.
- Study the career field in which you are interested.
- Understand your target audience.
- Become an expert in your field.
- Establish trust with your target audience.

Chapter 4

Communicating Over the Clutter

In This Chapter

- ◆ Keeping your message simple
- ◆ Communicating with your target audience
- ◆ Designing your unique visual brand
- ◆ Crafting your unique verbal brand

As you build your personal brand, getting your message to stand out from among the many other messages out there will be one of your biggest challenges. The advertising industry reports that the average consumer is bombarded with anywhere from 254 to 2,000 commercial messages each day.

Your challenge is to get your message to rise above the clutter. To get it noticed. In this chapter, you will be introduced to techniques that will help your messages stand out from the crowd. Clear, simple, and direct messaging is important, among all communication channels available.

The Struggle to Get Noticed

Today's key decision makers—whether you're attempting to get a job within a large corporation or seal a contract with a homeowner to paint his house—have very little time. They may scan applications, resumés, and proposals at an alarmingly fast rate. Your target audience may glance at an introductory e-mail, and never give it the attention that you feel it is due.

Talk to Your Audience

How can you get your message to stand out from the clutter? First, go back to one of the key elements of establishing your personal brand. Study the paths that will allow you to create a personal and emotional bond with your key audience. Do the people in your key audience read certain industry publications? If so, it may be possible to communicate with your key audience by writing a guest column about subjects they care about, or releasing media announcements about an award you have won. (See Chapter 10 for additional information regarding this type of communications.)

Begin thinking about ways your name will be recognized by others in your industry. Are you always on a list of award winners? Are you called to assist with industry-wide events? Do you participate in committees and commissions that oversee your field of interest? These are just a few ways to begin creating intimate bonds with your audience that will lead to career moves in the future.

Another way to establish an intimate bond is to get to know your target audience on a personal level. Call industry leaders and ask for advice. Go out of your way to speak with them after you've heard them talk at a national convention. Hand them your business card. Suggest setting up a meeting at their convenience so that you can ask a few questions about their company, their position, or the positions their company may have in the future. Attend conferences and meetings that will put you in contact with important people who are in your target audience. Schedule lunches every week or so with people you admire in your field. Attempt to have meetings with others who may lead to business opportunities for you.

By reaching out to others, you will begin to develop name recognition. Once people recognize your name, they will be more likely to read your letters or e-mail messages. Your target may accept your invitation to be LinkedIn, or befriend you on Facebook. You are now beginning to build a relationship that will boost you over the clutter of others.

Keep Your Message Simple

Everything about your brand should be relatively simple. In other words, you should be able to express your elevator pitch in a clear, concise manner anytime you bump into someone who asks you about your work. Your logo should be easy to understand. Your business card should be well designed and concise. No need to put all of your telephone numbers on it, if your cell phone number will do, for example.

Many people who have mega-brands started out with one simple area of expertise. Oprah Winfrey earned a notable reputation at first as a broadcast journalist and then as a talk-show host before she expanded her brand to include publishing and filmmaking. Martha Stewart ran a catering business out of the basement of her home before she grew into the mega-brand she is today.

Real World Brands

Oprah Winfrey started building her brand in 1971 at age 17 as a news reader at a Nashville, Tennessee, television station. When she was 22 she moved to Baltimore to be a news anchor and television reporter, but Winfrey was too emotional on camera. After just a few months, she became the co-host of a popular Baltimore morning show called *People Are Talking*.

Developing your branding story and your elevator pitch helps you focus on a clear message that explains your expertise. Everything from the layout of your resumé to the design of your website will affect your message. Your brand message, no matter what the niche you are attempting to fill, should simply and succinctly state your purpose.

Let the Creative Juices Flow

Brands that get noticed are those that incorporate the genius of imagination and creativity. *Brand immersion* occurs when a company creates an experience directed at its target audience.

We know a retired dentist who owned a vineyard. Instead of just opening a wine store next door, he created a brand immersion experience for his visitors. He offered wine tastings on a deck overlooking the vineyard. For a small fee, he invited customers to sample his wines along with cheese and crackers on the side. Instead of rushing through their tastings, his customers were able to sit back and enjoy the views, the food, and the wine. He sold a lot of cases of wine and built his personal brand as a wine expert in the process.

def•i•ni•tion

> **Brand immersion** occurs when customers get hands-on experience with the look and feel of a brand.

Your personal brand may get more recognition as you immerse yourself in your field of interest. In those cases, you can assimilate brand immersion by making a personal connection with your target audience. One young woman, desperate to work for Nike's corporate office, moved to Oregon and actively pursued the company's human resources department until she was given a shot at an interview. Armed with a degree in sports management, she aced multiple interviews and eventually landed a management position. During each interview, she talked about her hobbies—running and tennis—and exhibited a deep knowledge of the company's products and philosophy. She built her personal brand as being an athletic person who was living the Nike brand.

Personal brands that rise above the communication clutter will show your ability to spark a vivid connection with your target audience. Whether that's via a personal connection, a well-designed website, or an introductory e-mail that is concise and credible, the style you develop as your personal brand emerges will help you rise above the clutter and establish you as a true expert in your field.

Visual and Verbal Cues

Visual and verbal communication can do a lot for you as you establish your personal brand. These broad-ranging topics have to do with everything from the way you comb your hair (or don't) to how your voice message sounds. Ignoring the impact of your visual and verbal cues can have a negative impact on your personal brand.

Visual Identity

Your personal brand's visual identity is the part of you that is seen by others. It includes not only your physical appearance, but also your resumé, your website, your business card, and anything else that involves your brand.

First, allow us to address your appearance. If you are in a business that expects business attire in the workplace, of course you should meet that expectation. Don't be the lone employee who shows up with a tattoo and six piercings one Monday after a vacation at Venice Beach. If you're in a field that's more liberal in terms of dress and appearance, by all means, indulge yourself. We'll talk more about appearances in Chapter 8.

As you begin thinking about your personal brand, there are other elements that should be considered. For example, designing your resumé is of ultimate importance. Your business card should be a creation that reflects your personal brand—if you're artsy, it may reflect something cool and creative. If you're in the accounting business, it should be more straightforward. If you're a Realtor, you may want to put your picture on it so that you can create name and face recognition with future clients.

Known corporate brands go to great lengths to establish their visual identity. Take a look, for example, at the logo for Target. It's a simple, circular logo that is now easy to spot anywhere, even if the word *Target* is not with it. Notice that symbols, colors, and fonts selected for a logo are important to communicating a corporate strategy.

O, The Oprah Magazine is a perfect example of a personal branding mark. You only have to see the letter O, and you think of the magazine. Most people immediately recognize it as a creation of talk-show host Oprah Winfrey.

The same concepts apply to your personal brand. Think about the words, symbols, colors, and fonts that best express your personal brand. Consider your photo, if you plan to use it on your website or in a brochure. Is it professionally done and does it represent you in your best light? If you plan to incorporate illustrations into your brand identity, they should be carefully screened for quality.

Elements of Good Design

Elements of good design are especially important to keep in mind as you consider the printed materials you use to market your personal brand. Your resumé, of course, should be designed in a well-organized manner. We'll talk more about that in Chapter 5. But other items you may consider designing are vast: business cards, brochures, postcards, print advertisements, bulletin boards, posters, billboards, and more.

With the proliferation of desktop design and publishing software, more and more people are taking design into their own hands. While this gives people a great deal of freedom, it also means that too often the basic rules of design are ignored. We're not necessarily encouraging you to pay a designer to do all of your work for you, but if you opt to design your own marketing materials, you should become acquainted with some very basic rules of design.

Proximity

Proximity involves the way various elements are grouped together. For example, on your business card it is perhaps most visually appealing to group your contact information—such as telephone numbers and e-mail address—in one area so that a quick glance will tell your target exactly how they can reach you.

Although you might be tempted to try a more creative approach, such as putting each piece of information in a different corner of your business card, doing so may only serve to confuse your audience.

Alignment

Proper alignment means that information should look organized. Too many times we see clip art placed incongruously on a page just to fill space.

Nothing should be placed on the page without putting thought into it. A business card, for example, that looks haphazard and chaotic does not send the message that most people want to convey regarding their personal brands. Instead, you should strive to appear well organized, thoughtful, and smart.

Repetition

Good design often involves repetition. For example, use the same font for the subheads on your resumé. Use the same colors and borders throughout a brochure or advertisement. Repetition helps create a cohesive printed piece that is easy for your audience to read.

Contrast

Professional graphic designers use contrast in many ways, including their font styles, column sizes, colors, and graphics. For contrast to be effective, it should be distinct.

You can create contrast by using white type in a black box, for example. Or you can use contrasting fonts—such as a funky typeface like Chiller to promote a Halloween event with an informational typeface such as Times New Roman that provides the specific details of the event. For contrast to be attractive in design, there should be distinct and clear differences between elements that are put together.

White Space

Good designers know how to effectively use *white space*. White space is any space on a document that does not include text or graphics.

White space can be one of the most effective design features, offering a peaceful place for eyes to focus on amid the clutter. When used effectively, white space may enable your readers or viewers to better understand the message you are giving them. White space, in fact, can enhance the message of your text.

def•i•ni•tion

> **White space** is a graphic element that refers to open space on a page. This can refer to open space on your business card, on an advertisement, or on a poster. Generally, white space is considered to be a peaceful part of the design. It can have a dynamic impact by helping to focus attention on accompanying text or graphics.

Verbal Identity

Your verbal identity is just as important as your visual identity. The way you express yourself when talking to people will help establish good brand identity. No matter what your field of interest, your target audience expects you to be able to communicate clearly and concisely. You should use a professional tone of voice while expressing yourself in the best light possible to represent your personal brand.

For example, if you choose to add your own music to your voice-mail, that could be an important element if you're looking for a job as a musician. But if you're looking for a job in a bank, your target audience may think you're just wasting their time when they call you to leave a message.

Appropriate grammar and language skills are important as you establish this part of your brand's identity.

If you're in a field that frequently uses technical jargon—such as information technology or law—communicate with your target audience in layman's terms unless you are sure that they understand the technical terms. Choose the most concise and accurate language you can so that your target audience can easily understand you.

Talking too much can also be a problem. If your target stops making eye contact with you, take that as a clue that you may be talking too much. One more warning: don't be a conversation hijacker. If someone is in the midst of telling an enthralling story, don't steer the conversation back to yourself or your own experiences. Instead, take some time to ask additional questions to find out more about the person you're talking to.

One-on-One Communication

When you have one-on-one meetings with people in your field, be sure you have made your best effort to express yourself in ways that will assist you with creating an emotional bond.

As you begin meeting with people in your field of interest, here are a few tips to consider as you go about the task of having a productive conversation:

- Present yourself in the most positive way possible by dressing and behaving in a manner that fits the industry.

- Be armed with a list of questions you would like to know about the industry, the specific job or project, and the people with whom you will be working.

- Be flexible. If you ask a question and the answer brings another question to mind, feel free to ask it.

- When you are asked questions, express yourself in clear, simple language. Stay focused and try not to ramble. Many people say much more than they should when they are meeting someone for the first time.

- Make eye contact with the person to whom you are talking.

- Use body language that tells the person you are listening. This can be done by nodding or using other facial expressions.

- Avoid interrupting the person to whom you're listening.

- Humor is good as long as it's witty and not making fun of a particular person or group.

- Listen more than you talk.

- If you sense the meeting is coming to an end, express thanks.

Tips

Even though we are in an age of digital communication, sometimes it is simply more appropriate to take the time to handwrite a personal note. Stand apart from your peers and write heartfelt thank-you notes when the situation requires it.

The Least You Need to Know

- We are living in the gilded age of information.

- Keep your messages simple and direct.

- Your visual brand should follow simple design rules.

- Your verbal brand should include good grammar and clear, concise language.

Part 2

Launching Your Personal Brand

Now that you have written your personal branding story, examined your target audience, and learned the importance of communicating over the clutter, it's time to launch your personal brand. To do so, you will need to strategically communicate your message to your target audience.

To launch your personal brand, you must pay close attention to your resumé, other marketing collateral such as your business cards and brochures, as well as your social connections and networks.

Chapter 5

Brand Identity: Starting with Your Resumé

In This Chapter

- ◆ Using your brand identity to create your resumé
- ◆ Designing the best visual cues
- ◆ Creating your portfolio
- ◆ Writing a cover letter

Your personal brand identity is the visual and verbal way you present yourself. Consider, for example, the well-known brand of Ben & Jerry's Ice Cream. It's easy to recognize Ben & Jerry's in the ice-cream freezer at your local grocery store because its visual packaging stands out. As Ben & Jerry's established its visual identity, the company chose an image of a spotted Jersey cow. That image, as well as the unique verbal cues used in naming their products—consider Cherry Garcia ice cream named after the late Grateful Dead guitarist Jerry Garcia—have helped Ben & Jerry's establish a strong corporate brand.

A graphic designer we know has done a superb job of branding herself. She has created a large, colorful and bold flower that appears on her website, on her business cards, and on the packets that she mails out to potential clients. The flower says that she loves color, good design, and being bold. It's all about her design style, as well as her personal brand.

One person will not need to do the massive work that most corporations do to establish brand identities. Yet there are some important avenues to consider as you introduce your brand to the world. Now that you have learned the basic skills for visual and verbal cues, put them to test by considering the elements needed as you begin to launch your personal brand.

Basic Resumé Design

As you begin to communicate your brand identity to others through your resumé, consider your target audience. Will your resumé be directed to a potential employer, potential clients, or possible partners or funders who will assist you with an entrepreneurial endeavor?

The first time many people in your target market consider your brand, they may be looking at your professional resumé. Making your resumé visually appealing is of utmost importance. But how do you do that? The following information will help you develop a new resumé or reconsider an existing one to make sure that your brand is clearly defined.

Tips

Basic design elements are also important for your resumé. Once you organize your material in a well-structured format, consider the elements of proximity, alignment, contrast, and repetition. Skipping lines between subheads will provide your reading audience with a necessary rest.

Consider your resumé's style, including the visual cues you have put into play. Is your name in a font that is strong and readable? Are fonts consistent throughout? Is your resumé well organized, emphasizing facts that distinguish you from your peers?

Get Organized

Organize the information so that your name and contact information is at the very top of the page.

Other categories you choose to include will probably be the following:

- Your Mission—a short sentence or two that will completely focus your professional goal

- Professional Experience

- Education

- Awards & Honors

- Publications

- Special Skills

- Activities & Organizations

Generally, all items on your resumé are going to be listed from the most recent experience first to the oldest experience last. This makes a resumé easy to scan and size up for those who are in your target market.

Take some time to think through your targeted priorities. First, consider the positions or clients or investors that you are trying to impress. What are your outstanding attributes that will make a lasting impression on your target audience?

Begin organizing those attributes in a rough draft. Have you had a lot of experience in your field of interest? If so, let your experience speak for itself. If not, emphasize the experiences you have had that fit the needs of your target audience. Keep in mind that it is not necessary to share all of your work experiences with your target audience. Only share the experiences in which you have gained skills that will make you more valuable to your target.

As you begin your personal branding effort, you will want to pull out the information that is unrelated to the brand you are attempting to build. For example, if you are a recent college graduate attempting to brand yourself as an expert in public relations, now is the time to eliminate the work experience at the local video store while in high school.

What is more relevant, perhaps, would be volunteer work you've done promoting various campus organizations. Here is a resumé that reflects a new graduate's goal of being hired by a corporate retail firm:

Levi Lynn
100 Eli Ave.
Allston, MA 02134
(740) 973-0000
llynn@gmail.com

Objective

To obtain a full-time position using my superior organizational and creative skills in a corporate retail environment.

Experience

2006–present   The Body Shop   **Boston, MA**

Lead cashier (excellent costumer service skills, training abilities, loss prevention experience, visual and creative talents). General clerk.

Summer 2008   Auction.net   **Barcelona, Spain**

Interned at international technology firm that designs auction websites. Completed research, designed logo, and wrote white paper. Clarified English grammar for website text and other company communications.

2006–2008   The Body Shop   **Columbus, OH**

Worked as cashier during college breaks, including summers prior to 2008.

2006–2007   Nike Tennis Camp   **Granville, OH**

Taught tennis and served as part-time secretary for the Peter Burling Tennis Camp at Denison University.

Summer 2005   Denison University   **Granville, OH**
            Public Affairs

Wrote press releases for newspapers nationwide and performed secretarial duties in the Office of Public Affairs.

Education

2005–present   Boston University   **Boston, MA**
2001–2005   Granville High School   **Granville, OH**

Internships and Extracurriculars

Fall 2007 **Internship at Calgery Gallery** **Boston, MA**
on Newberry St.

Assisted with general gallery care one afternoon each week.

Fall 2005 **Boston University-After** **Boston, MA**
School Program

Volunteered one day a week at a Catholic elementary school in
Jamaica Plains to help children with homework and activities
planned in this after-school program.

Avoid overly-long resumés. Be sure yours is just long enough to show
items that will help show off your brand and your experiences. Below is
the resumé of a health-care worker who specializes in respiratory issues
and has built an international brand.

Patricia B. Koff
100 Dolomite Dr.
Colorado Springs, CO 80919
719-494-0000
pbkoff@hotmail.com

Summary: Respiratory health-care provider with clinical, management,
education, and fundraising skills. Has extensive international experience and is currently actively redesigning chronic health-care delivery.

EXPERIENCE
University of Colorado Hospital, Denver, CO
Program Coordinator (Jan. 2006–present)
Responsible for development and implementation of
a service program using information technology and
medical equipment for 500+ participants with COPD.
* Integrated eHealth for COPD
* Organized public relations events and spirometry screenings
* Liaison for primary care offices
* Developed research protocol and obtained related equipment

Coordinator for New Care Initiative (Oct. 2003–Dec. 2005).
Responsibilities included development and support of
programs/projects related to chronic care improvement—
modeled from Medicare initiative.
   * Developed model for characterization of COPD
     health care within UCH

University of Barcelona-Hospital Clinic, Barcelona, Spain
Servei de Pneumologia (Aug. 2002–June 2003).
Responsible for support of European Union–funded projects for
CHRONIC (deliverables, public relations, proposals)

Penrose Community Hospital, Colorado Springs, CO
Respiratory Therapist (Feb. 2001–Aug. 2002).
Provided care in adult, pediatric, neonatal, and emergency care
areas. Also performed electrocardiograms and set up home
cardiac monitoring.

University of Colorado Health Sciences Center, Denver, CO
Development Coordinator, Division of Pulmonary Sciences and
Critical Care Medicine and University of Colorado Foundation
(1992–94)

*Director of Respiratory Care Services and Gastrointestinal
Center* at University Hospital (1989–90)

Pediatric Coordinator for Respiratory Care (1987–88)

EDUCATION
Master's Degree in Health Occupations Education, University of
Florida (1982)
Bachelor's Degree in Health Sciences, University of Florida
(1980)

INTERNATIONAL VOLUNTEER EXPERIENCE
Bolivia (June 2001). Provided health-care instruction at
clinics in San Ignacio De Valesco, Bolivia.

East Meets West Foundation (Dec. 1999). Provided health-care
instruction to school children in Danang, Vietnam.

St. Petersburg, Russia (Feb.–Sept. 1996). Coordinated prenatal
health-care services for American clinic in Russia, including
delivery plans in Finland, Western Europe, and the USA.

AWARDS
Colorado Society for Respiratory Care Practitioner of the Year (1995)
American Association for Respiratory Care President's Recognition
(1988,89)
American Association for Respiratory Care Outstanding Pediatric
Practitioner (1985)

PUBLICATIONS
Koff, Westfall: "Telemedicine and Chronic Obstructive Pulmonary
Disease" in *Chronic Obstructive Lung Diseases,* 2nd edition by Voelkel
and MacNee. BC Decker Inc, 2008 (in press – scheduled for publication May 2008).

Koff P, Stevens C, Cashman J, Greene K, Jones R, Vandivier R,
Voelkel N, "Telemonitoring/eHealth management improves quality of
life and healthcare expenditures in COPD." *Am J Respir Crit Care Med*
2006;3;A123.

Hernandez C, Casas A, Marti D, Estrada D, Fernandez J, Olmos C, Koff
P, Barbera JA, Rodriguez-Roisin R., Roca J. "Effects of Multidisciplinary
Home-Based Intervention in Preventing Hospitalizations in COPD
Patients: A Randomized Controlled Study." *Am J Respir Crit Care Med*
2003;167 (7):A747.

DesJardins, Koff: *Neonatal/Pediatric Respiratory Care Pocket Card and
Manual,* Dubuque: Simon & Kolz Publishing, 1998.

Neonatal and Pediatric Respiratory Care (The Video and Workbook
Series), St. Louis: Mosby-Year Book, Inc., A Times Mirror Company,
1995.

What Is Your Goal?

One young lady, an associate producer for a major television talk show,
wanted to do more work as a writer. On her resumé, she wanted to
emphasize her experience contributing to publications, in addition to
her television work. Thus, she developed a section on her resumé under
the heading "Publications," where she listed the name of the article that
she wrote for a college alumni publication and her photo procurement
work for a travel book.

As you're developing your resumé, your current goal is the most important part of it. If you have been an elementary school teacher, but you are currently opening a tutoring business, your resumé should emphasize your years in education along with any accreditation and awards that you received. It is your dedication to students that will help sell your tutoring business. In other words, running a tutoring business is more about selling your skills. If you were looking for a job teaching school, your years of experience would be more important.

Consider your personal branding story and how your resumé should be organized to help you achieve the maximum results, whether that's being called in for a job interview, being approved for a loan to start a business, or getting a major company to agree that you're the best private contractor available to do their internal heating and air conditioning service. Your resumé speaks for you when you are not in the room.

Your Experiences

Experiences are important whether or not you get paid for them. If you're just entering the job market, the work experiences related to your field of interest may be scarce. If that's the case, feel free to list related internships or other unpaid experiences that you may have had during your college years.

The same applies if you are older but are trying to develop a new brand for yourself: use any experiences—whether paid or unpaid—that are related to the current area of interest.

Generally, resumés should highlight your most recent experience first and then list other experiences in backward, chronological order, such as noted in the sidebar.

The professional experience in the following resumé is for someone who moved from Ohio to California and wanted to land a job in the California school system. She tailored her resumé to emphasize her experience organizing conferences as well as her training and grant-writing skills. She eventually landed a position at a California technical school administering a grant aiming to increase Hispanic enrollment.

Professional Experience:

Consultant & Intermittent Employee, Ohio Department of Education

2007–2008	Economic and Education Summit Coordinator
2002–2007	Ohio School Improvement Institute Coordinator
2006–2007	Leadership and Policy Forum Coordinator, N.E. Ohio High Schools That Work Special Projects
1999–2000	High Schools That Work and Equity Projects
1994–1999	Equity Consultant, The Ohio State University
1997, 1996	New Team Evaluator and Trainer
1995	Nontraditional Workshop Coordinator

Branding Marks: Awards and Such

If you have won awards in your field of interest, have received special designations from community organizations, or have special skills in areas that most people don't, then these can become the branding marks that help differentiate you in the marketplace. In the case of your personal brand, consider a branding mark a specific achievement that makes you stand out from the crowd of others in your field.

Be sure to list such accomplishments in your resumé. Generally, such accolades are listed in an area called "Awards or Skills" after the "Experience and Education" section.

Readability

Keep in mind that this chapter has a lot to do with the visual and verbal cues that you are sending your target audience. Thus, pay close attention to the readability of your resumé, in terms of both the words and phrases you have selected as well as the typography.

Warning

If ever there was a case for having someone proofread a piece of your work, this is it. With spell check on most word processing programs, it's easy to skip over the proofreading process. Words may be missing or completely wrong for the sentence that they appear in. For example, the word "too" will be approved by a spell-checking program when you mean to use the word "to."

Be careful to thoroughly check your spelling for each and every word on your resumé before you send it off to your target audience.

Accountability and Accuracy

Make sure your resumé is accurate and up-to-date. Do not make the assumption, as many people do, that they can pad their length of employment, hide the fact that they recently lost a job, or plug in an award where none really existed. This is part of brand authenticity that we introduced in Chapter 2.

Here's an example that didn't turn out so well for the job applicant. Sherry recently served on a committee formed to hire the executive director of a health organization. This was a high-level job opportunity with a six-figure salary. Interviews were scheduled with at least six candidates, and members of the committee met with each for nearly two hours. One candidate appeared to be highly experienced and likable. Coming from another part of the state, however, no one on the committee was familiar with him. His experiences were good, according to his resumé, and he spoke the language of a long-time health-care executive.

Nonetheless, there was a concern that the committee just didn't quite know enough about him. Committee members called the applicant's references, and they all checked out. However, a quick Google search revealed that the man's current title and place of employment—administrator at a small hospital—was obsolete. The hospital had gone out of business just months earlier. Not once during the interview did the job candidate insinuate that he was unemployed, that the hospital was closed, or that his job had disappeared. His resumé was quickly sent to the recycling bin.

Remember, we're in an era of constant information proliferation. Authenticity matters. People will find out if you're not truthful. A quick Google or Yahoo! Internet search can reveal a newspaper article or other information that will quickly blow your cover. Be honest when asked, and don't make it apparent that you're trying to cover up a job loss or something similar.

An Introductory Letter

When you send your resumé to a target audience, you will want to include a professional cover letter. Whether you are sending your resumé via e-mail or snail mail, a cover letter is a way to introduce yourself to your audience and to touch on your basic areas of expertise.

Your cover letter should be set up as a formal letter. If you are e-mailing your resumé to your target, you will want to attach your cover letter to a brief e-mail that says something like: *Attached, you will find a cover letter and resumé that I'm submitting in response to your recent advertisement.* You may also want to add a second sentence that summarizes why you stand out from the crowd: *I have won five national awards from the American Marketing Association and look forward to talking to you about your current opening.*

Your professional cover letter will be longer than that brief e-mail. Your first paragraph may be similar to the above, but you'll want to add a few more details about your experience and enthusiasm for the currently open position.

The final paragraph in your cover letter should be considered a call to action. This is a marketing and sales term that refers to a statement made that will help spur your target audience into action. Your final paragraph may say something such as:

My resumé is attached. Please let me know if I can provide additional information. I will call you on Monday, Jan. 24, if I do not hear from you before then. Thank you for your consideration.

Your Resumé vs. Your Website

You should not assume that having a personal website will replace sending a resumé to your target audience. We are not, as a society, to the point that your website, Facebook, or MySpace page will replace the professional resumé.

Nonetheless, you may find it very convenient to create a basic professional website. Again, we'll discuss the specifics of your personal website in Chapter 11.

The Importance of a Portfolio

Creating a portfolio of your work is important in a variety of professions.

Choosing Your Portfolio Case

Portfolios can vary greatly in size and content. Your portfolio should portray what is unique about you. Depending on your career field, your work can range from pieces of artwork or design work to published articles. Avoid including term papers or anything that all college students produce. The goal of accumulating a portfolio of your work is to display your uniqueness and how you may fit your target audience's professional needs.

You can get notebook-size portfolio cases at most office supply stores or large, art-size portfolios at art supply stores. Generally, you should have enough pages to show 12 to 20 pieces of your work.

Design Options

Your portfolio should focus on your work with few embellishments. On the first page, you will want to include an introduction to yourself—a couple of paragraphs that focus on your work, your goals, and your experience. Or you could simply put a copy of your resumé on the first page.

What you put in the rest of the portfolio depends on your area of expertise. If you are an event planner, for example, you may want to include invitations, RSVP cards, photos of actual events you have planned, and news clippings about those events. If you work in marketing, you should include collateral from a marketing campaign you designed, such as a business card, an invitation, a brochure, a newsletter, a copy of an electronic newsletter, an advertisement, etc. (You can get more ideas regarding collateral when we discuss that in Chapter 6.)

Whatever you choose to put into your portfolio, make sure that it is of high professional quality—from its design to its printing—as you will be competing with others who are showing professional-quality work.

The Least You Need to Know

- ◆ Your branding story will help you create your resumé.
- ◆ Your resumé should be organized to reflect your goals.
- ◆ Your portfolio should include your resumé, news stories, and collateral that reflects your brand.

Chapter 6

Effective Messaging: Creating Collateral

In This Chapter

- ◆ Making your messages meaningful
- ◆ Branding your business card
- ◆ Creating marketing collateral that accentuates your brand
- ◆ Communicating your brand through touch and feel

As the world's communication methods have multiplied, so have the vast array of possibilities to spread the word about yourself and your brand. Effective messaging means that you are paying close attention to the verbal and visual elements of your personal brand. This chapter will help you carefully examine the types of marketing collateral available to assist you in communicating your brand to your target audience.

Marketing collateral varies from basic business cards to billboards and everything in between. In this chapter, we offer some basic tips and solutions to creating the collateral you need, without breaking the bank.

What Do You Really Need?

Because of the various communication channels available today—ranging from old-school methods such as basic business cards to today's web and cell-phone options—there is always someone trying to sell us something we do not need. Pay copious attention to the details of your marketing collateral and determine what best suits your target audience. Keep and mind that this will vary, depending on who your target audience is.

Your Business Card

Almost everyone in almost every profession can benefit from a business card that is succinct and provides basic contact information.

A sample business card, front (top) and back (bottom).

Your business card should include your name, the name of your company (if applicable), a line about services offered (if clarification is necessary), and your contact information, including your telephone numbers, e-mail address, and website. If you are a recent college graduate looking for your first professional position, a business card with your name, address, and contact information will, at the least, show your target audience that you have the skills and motivation necessary to produce such a card for yourself. It will also make you stand out from the crowd, as most college students don't consider such options.

Another sample business card, front (top) and back (bottom).

Office supply stores and several online websites offer good deals on 500 to 1,000 basic business cards. Order a limited quantity if you are just starting out in your career, as you may find that your brand evolves and that you'll want to reprint your business cards within a year or two.

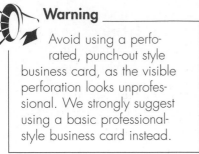

Warning

Avoid using a perforated, punch-out style business card, as the visible perforation looks unprofessional. We strongly suggest using a basic professional-style business card instead.

Preformatted business cards offered by office supply stores, print shops, and online sites produce fine basic products if you are on a limited budget and just starting out. You can browse various basic designs either online or by looking at a catalog that most office supply stores or print shops have available.

Even though they're more expensive, it's a good investment to order a custom-designed card that includes your personal logo, if you have one, and in some cases your photograph or other artwork. If you're a professional who owns a business of your own, we encourage you to consider working with a graphic designer you know, or one recommended by your local printer, to create such a card.

Your Signature Line

One of the easiest and most visible virtual marketing tools is one that many people overlook: your e-mail signature line.

As you establish your personal brand, take advantage of the signature line that you can set up to be automatically added to the end of each e-mail you send. Because e-mail is frequently used when you're trying to communicate with your target audience, it's an easy way to introduce your brand.

Your signature line, of course, will include your full name. But a signature line can include more than one line of text. It may include your title—if you have one—and your company name.

If you are just starting out in your personal branding effort, your signature line may look something like this:

Robert Smith
Outdoor Wildlife Photographer
www.wildrob.com
(919) 323-6666

or

Julie Jamison, Proprietor
Fresh Berry Preserves
www.JuliesJelly.com
(314) 660-0000

Your signature line may include your address, your telephone number(s), and your website address. Generally, it is not necessary to include your e-mail address in your signature line as your target will already have that accessible since you are sending it via e-mail.

A signature line is an oft-overlooked way of marketing yourself with every e-mail you send out. We know many experienced authors, for example, who tag the name of their newest book on their signature line. They may also add a niche-specific blog address and other pertinent information. Here's a good current example:

Sandra Gurvis
614-555-5555
www.sgurvis.com
www.theflowerchildrenbook.com
www.booksaboutthe60s.com
Author of: THE PIPE DREAMERS and
WHERE HAVE ALL THE FLOWER CHILDREN GONE?

If you haven't yet created a signature line for your personal brand, think about doing it as soon as possible. It's an easy and free way of letting your target audience know about you.

Other Marketing Pieces That Accentuate Your Brand

Marketing collateral extends far beyond your business card as you go about creating your personal brand.

Letterhead

You can accentuate your personal brand by designing or working with a graphic designer to create unique letterhead for your formal communications. Letterhead can easily be created on a Word document with a choice of fonts and then reproduced on a basic business-size envelope in the form of a return address. A basic, consistent letterhead design emphasizes your personal, professional brand.

Consider the example, below, created on a Word document:

Adam Smith	
310 E. Cambridge Ave.	(518) 882-0000
Smithville, NY 20008	asmith@alltel.com

Postcards

A postcard is a quick, inexpensive method of staying in touch. Your local printer or office supply store can produce postcards for you. Let's say that you have met someone of prominence at a local chamber of commerce meeting or another gathering. A quick follow-up note on your branded postcard is a perfect way to touch base after an event.

Unless you're artistically inclined yourself, hire a local printer or a graphic designer to help you add a few basic graphic elements that will make your postcard stand out in a pile of mail. If you decide to add graphics, be sure that they represent a clear image that fits your brand. Keep in mind that in this age of virtual everything, a handwritten note may endear you to your target audience.

Brochures

Take a basic 8.5×11-inch piece of paper and fold it in half, horizontally. This is an example of a very basic brochure. Start over with a whole sheet of paper and tri-fold it. Now you have a second example.

Some people see brochures as too costly to produce when you are just starting your personal brand. But if you're starting a business such as Julie Jamison's Jellies, mentioned earlier, a brochure will help your target audience understand exactly what you offer. A brochure is a piece of marketing collateral that can offer a fuller picture about you and your brand.

A postcard (front and back) can be a great way to market yourself.

If you have developed a logo to represent your personal brand, include it on the front of your brochure. You will also want to include basic biographical information about yourself, your company (if you have one), and the products and services you offer. Be sure to include your website address and all of your contact information.

Again, your local printing company or a variety of online websites can help you create a cost-efficient and professional customized brochure.

A Marketing Kit

A marketing kit is a packet of information about your brand that you can assemble to distribute to your target audience. Musical bands, small businesses, and others assemble marketing kits to get the word out about themselves.

As you develop your personal brand, there may be occasions in which a marketing kit will be helpful. For instance, it might be the sort of thing you bring to a chamber of commerce luncheon in order to introduce your brand to local business people. Or you may want to consider mailing your marketing kits to key people in your industry.

At minimum, you will want a good, basic pocket folder that will last for a few years in someone's file drawer. Avoid the cheapest folders, and go for something more substantial instead. If your budget can support it, talk to your local printer about the possibility of creating a special folder that sports your logo and pertinent information.

The graphic designer we mentioned previously created a basic white folder that featured a special cut (called a dye cut) on its outside flap resembling the colorful flower she uses as part of her logo. It is a unique folder that stands out from the crowd. Talk to your local printer if you want to explore the possibility of custom creating a folder specific to your brand.

Inside a marketing folder, you'll want to assemble items such as your resumé or a personal bio; fact sheets about you, your company, or your products and services; your brochure; and copies of any news clippings that pertain to your brand.

Most people creating a personal brand will probably not need a poster. However, there are some circumstances in which creating posters will be helpful, such as when you're running for public office or advertising your musical band. A poster can be a cost-efficient method of communicating your personal brand. A real estate agent, for example, may want to create an 8.5×11-inch page that promotes a certain house for sale in a particular neighborhood. Put this information onto some cardstock and, voilà, a quick poster is born. Posters can range in size up from a regular notebook page to those much larger.

Bulletin Boards

There are some obvious situations—such as when you're running for political office or selling real estate, golf clubs, jewelry, and the like—when incorporating a bulletin board into your marketing plan may be very helpful.

If you are an artist who displays his or her pottery at a local coffee shop, you may have the chance to use a bulletin board on site to tell a little about your branding story, show a few pictures about the way you work, and provide your contact information, price list, and a schedule of your shows.

As with your portfolio, you'll want to be sure that the bulletin board is professionally designed.

Warning

Avoid any tendency to do a half-professional job on any marketing tool. It's better to go without a business card, brochure, or bulletin board than to distribute something that reflects poorly on your brand by being poorly designed.

Billboards

We know a local real estate agent who posts her photograph on regional billboards in a larger-than-life method of promoting her brand. Certainly, it's a surefire way of standing out from her competition. Our real estate friend is a good example of someone who thinks outside the box in ways to promote her personal brand.

Although billboards certainly aren't appropriate for every personal brand, they can be a cost-effective way of advertising your brand if you have a target audience that drives by every day. For real estate agents, bankers, politicians, and others, billboards are a viable marketing method. Don't rule them out as a potential marketing tool as you put together a drive-by plan to target your audience with your personal brand. We'll discuss this option in more detail in Chapter 13 when we discuss paid advertising.

As your personal brand grows, your marketing collateral can take on many forms, shapes, and sizes. If you are an independent artist, you may eventually produce a catalog of your branded products. If you are importing scarves from Europe, your marketing collateral may involve the branded boxes in which you ship them. As you begin exercising your personal brand and get to know your target audience on a more intimate level, various opportunities for producing marketing collateral will be made available to you. We emphasize that you carefully select collateral that connects well with your target audience. The goal here is to build a stronger brand, not just to stand out from the crowd.

The Least You Need to Know

- ◆ Marketing collateral involves your business card, brochures, posters, and other such materials that help promote our brand.

- ◆ Your e-mail's signature line can promote your brand with every e-mail you write.

- ◆ Effective messaging means that you follow basic visual and verbal cues that help you communicate your brand.

- ◆ Carefully consider the habits of your target audience when creating your marketing collateral.

Chapter 7

Developing Brand Associations

In This Chapter

- Building a brand through partnerships
- Branding through social networking channels
- Establishing associations in the workplace by joining professional organizations
- Building associations in your community by getting involved in groups
- Taking a leadership position

What people and groups are you linked with? Your reputation is shaped in large part by the people with whom you spend time. The more powerful your associations, the more powerful you will appear to be. The more credible your associations, the more credible you will appear to be.

A term marketing professionals use is *halo effect*. It deals with how perception influences consumers. A positive response to one product or service by your company can carry over to other services and goods you carry. For example, the strong feeling people have toward Coke will carry over to other Coca-Cola beverages.

Companies also try to enhance their brands by linking them with other brands. General Motors sponsored the TV broadcast of the Oscars from 1998 to 2008, spending about $110 million, according to press accounts. Businesses coughed up $2.7 million to $3 million for a 30-second commercial during the Super Bowl. Hilton, the hotel chain, features Crabtree and Evelyn toiletries in its bathrooms. The message: associating with high-profile, popular, top-of-the-line events, businesses, and products can enhance a brand's reputation.

Perceptions and Power

You can apply this same concept—on a much smaller scale—to your personal brand.

Tips

For young professionals just starting their careers, your brand will be strengthened if you begin to associate more with your work colleagues instead of heading back to your college hangouts.

Who are you hanging out with? Which company do you work for or take on as a client?

If you can get access to powerful people, either through business contacts or volunteering, the more value your brand will have. The fewer people between you and the decision makers, the more prestige and the more power you will have.

And by power we mean the ability to get things done, to persuade people to rally around your point of view. You persuade people by making strong arguments and building trust. People trust you once they get to know you.

By building a strong personal brand, you become someone that others want to work with or for. People are attracted to high-quality, trustworthy, and consistent leaders. For example, we know of a personal trainer who works with wealthy clients, including a celebrity who happens to have a summer home in the area. These associations definitely enhance his brand. In fact, he has developed such strong relationships with his clients that a few of them have backed him financially so he can open his own gym.

The rest of the chapter will explore ways to make associations that will strengthen your brand.

Be a People Person

To get your brand linked with other brands, you have to get involved. The best way to do this is by becoming active in your community. Get involved in your community so people realize who you are, what you do, and what value you can bring to their lives.

We know a successful developer who is long past retirement age. But he still works because he loves his job. He has power and influence at a high level. He knows how to get things done largely because he knows the people who can get things done. He is seen as a valuable civic member.

He prides himself on knowing as many people as possible. He's polite and respectful and he's a relentless people person. At parties and other social events, he circulates constantly, shaking hands, making small talk, always smiling. By the end of the evening, he's probably talked to everyone in the room, making new contacts and reaffirming old ones. He's known as Mr. Charm, the man who knows everyone. That's not a bad brand to have.

Tips

Even something as trivial as the ring tone of your cell phone can influence how people perceive your brand. A silly or inappropriate ring tone could send the message that you shouldn't be taken seriously or are immature. So give some thought to how your brand is affected when you receive a call on your cell phone.

Old-School Social Networking

Online social networking is getting a lot of attention these days—and we devote a couple of chapters later in this book to building relationships via the web—but it is still vitally important to actually meet people:

shake hands, smile, look them in the eye, talk directly with them. Building personal relationships in person still matters.

A key to making new contacts is the art of the quick conversation. One way to make a good impression is to focus the attention on the other person. Ask the other person about him- or herself. People like to talk about themselves, and your approach will show that you are curious. After your brief encounter, chances are they likely will leave with a positive memory of your discussion. At the same time, you should contribute a few things to the discussion so it doesn't feel as if you are a detective interrogating a suspect.

In almost any conversation with someone new, you will be asked about what you do. People don't want to be bored with details or struggle to understand a vague description. Be prepared to give a concise, specific answer. Now's the time to bring out that brief elevator pitch you prepared in Chapter 2. Some are easy: I'm an accountant. Or I work in an accounting firm that figures out how to save other companies money. I'm a village planner. Or I work with village leaders and residents on how to improve everyone's quality of life.

Remember to pass out your business card, and also ask for one. And once you get home or back to the office, enter the information into your contact database right away to avoid misplacing the card.

One trick to meeting new people is to go to an event by yourself. If other people attend the event with you, you will tend to congregate with them. Sure, you may feel uncomfortable showing up by yourself, but it will force you to start a conversation with other people and to avoid that uneasy sensation of standing by yourself during a social occasion.

Start building a "portfolio" of anecdotes—stories you can tell to people you meet for the first time, ones you can wheel out in a speech or when you're at a dinner party.

Real World Brands

One of the personal characteristics that got a lot of attention when George Herbert Walker Bush won the presidential election in 1988 was his habit of writing notes to people he met. He credited it with helping to build many relationships in his life. That personal touch is unusual, memorable, and effective.

Building Associations at Work

Where you work says something about you. If you worked for Enron in the 1990s, you were seen as part of a successful, innovative company. If you worked for the company in the early 2000s, you were seen as part of a corrupt, greedy culture.

What is the brand of the department you work in? Does it get things done? Or does it miss deadlines? Your personal brand is shaped by that association. If you are in a department with a bad brand, you'll need to work to improve the brand (and hopefully get credit for doing so) or move to a different division within your company.

Who is your boss? Even if you don't like your boss, your brand is hitched to your boss's star. There may be times you need to make your boss look good so you can look good.

Join Professional Associations

Every profession has an association that represents its interest (such as bar associations for lawyers) and those groups have local chapters. Whether you're a marketer, a doctor, or a plumber, find people who do the same work and who meet regularly.

If there isn't a group, start your own. Advertise for members to gather at a coffee shop and go from there.

Attend Professional Conferences

A good way to meet people of similar interests and build contacts in your industry is to go to professional conferences. But take it one step further. Join a committee or even try to take a leadership role in planning the events. You will make valuable contacts who can help advance your career.

Invite Contacts to Lunch or Breakfast

Try to avoid eating lunch at your desk. Make lunch appointments with business associates, people you just met, or even someone you heard speak whom you would like to get to know better. Perhaps they will turn you down, but maybe they will say yes.

Become a Board Member

Organizations and businesses need people to help oversee their operations. Publicly traded companies have boards that need people to help guide the executives. Nonprofits have boards to help their leaders. You can have an impact on an organization—whether it's the local community theater or a large corporation. And your performance will be witnessed by key people who talk to other key people.

Join the Media

We will explore this topic in more detail in Chapter 9, but think about how to build your brand through associating yourself with the media.

Consider hosting a radio show, becoming a reliable source for reporters covering your area of expertise, or writing a column for the local paper. Getting your name in the media can build visibility and credibility.

Speak, Publicly

If you are an expert in a particular area, you are a candidate to talk at conferences. It's a good way to start establishing some recognition for yourself. It's not easy, of course, and many people aren't comfortable with standing in front of others and trying to be entertaining and informative.

Tips

Are you uncomfortable speaking in front of large audiences? Start taking steps to overcome that fear. Join the local chapter of Toastmasters International or hire a speaking coach.

Brand Associations in the Community

One major way to build a brand association is through goodwill in the community. How can you give back to others to try to improve your neighborhood, city, state, or country?

Doing good also can be good for business. If you are an important part of a respected organization, you will be viewed in a favorable light. Your brand will be connected to another good brand.

One way is to volunteer. We know a real estate agent who joined a civic group because he was interested in making contacts to advance his career. He ended up running a number of projects. In the end, he built many strong personal *and* professional relationships by doing a lot of good.

So volunteer for something you care about and that you can contribute to. You will begin to develop a network of people who trust you and will turn to you when they need help in your area of expertise.

If you want to build a brand, to stand out from the crowd, to make a difference, then you have to build personal relationships by putting yourself in situations where you can rub shoulders with people who can help you build your personal brand. Here are some ideas for getting started.

Get Political

There are plenty of opportunities to get involved in politics, from the grassroots to the national level. Every campaign needs volunteers to make phone calls or stuff envelopes.

This is a great way to make a big impression quickly. Campaigns need passionate people who will work long hours to do whatever needs done. There are plenty of stories of volunteers who have impressed the right people and have gone on to become campaign leaders or even candidates themselves.

Help Out at Your Church

Churches survive on volunteers. Bring your expertise to the table, whether it's writing the church newsletter or sitting on the construction committee for a new addition.

Coach Your Kid's Team

There are always opportunities to get involved in recreation programs. Start coaching a kids' team. If you don't know the sport, get an instructional video or read a book. Coaching is not supposed to be about teaching them to be pros, but helping them learn a few things, keeping them organized, and making sure somebody is in charge of bringing the snacks for each game.

Those kids have parents who will get to know what kind of person you are by how you handle their children. When they see how well you can deal with a dozen little kids—all with different personalities—you can make a good impression. Besides, it can be a lot of fun.

Show Up for Your Child's Activity

When our daughter played soccer in middle school, we were at first hesitant. Do we really want to be soccer parents—consume our weekends traveling across the city to spend the day at a field watching a bunch of kids running around playing a game we didn't really understand?

It didn't take long for us to begin enjoying our weekend forays to the soccer fields. One of the big reasons was the bond we formed with the other parents. We looked forward to standing on the sideline cheering for the girls and talking with the other mothers and fathers. We got to know a lot of interesting people with whom we became friends. People got to know us.

After a couple of years of playing, our daughter announced she didn't want to play soccer anymore. We tried to talk her out of quitting because we thought the exercise was good for her. She shot back, "The only reason you want me to play is so you can hang out with your friends." We both realized she was partially right.

Help Out at School

Join a parent-teacher organization and take a responsibility that interests you. Volunteer in the classroom, if possible. Participate in a public school levy (if your community votes on them to fund its educational district) or support a school board candidate.

Warning

Keep in mind that political ventures can be controversial and divisive. But if you believe in the cause and listen to all the arguments respectfully while advocating for your side, you can build goodwill—and a reputation for being a fair player.

Join Your Neighborhood Group

Most neighborhoods have an organization that meets with city government to represent its interests. What if your streets need paved or the sewers back up in rainstorms? What if the speed limits on neighborhood streets are too high? The association can lobby public officials for action.

You can be part of that lobbying effort. You will be working on a worthwhile cause while meeting key government contacts. If you are chosen president, you become the face of your neighborhood.

Real World Brands

Toastmasters International is an organization dedicated to helping people hone their communication and leadership skills. Its distinguished alumni include Pete Coors of Coors Brewing Company; Debbi Fields, the founder of Mrs. Fields Cookies; Tom Peters, the noted author and management expert; and Linda Lingle, the governor of Hawaii.

Volunteer at Charitable Events

Most nonprofit organizations need to do fundraising to survive. They need help in pulling off the events, from setting up tables to recruiting donors to raising money.

These events bring together a number of people who are passionate about their particular cause.

The point is that it doesn't really matter how you make contacts in your community, you just need to start doing it. If you are dedicated and dependable, you will begin to generate a positive buzz about your brand.

The Least You Need to Know

◆ Making personal contact is the best way to build trust.

◆ Join organizations for the right reasons, not just to help your business.

◆ Learn more about the person you're conversing with and talk less about yourself.

◆ Build a database of new contacts.

◆ Reach out to people you don't know by sending notes or inviting them to lunch.

Chapter 8

The Total Experience: Living Your Brand

In This Chapter

- ◆ Making a good first impression
- ◆ Knowing your manners
- ◆ Interacting in a personal way
- ◆ Hosting and sponsoring social events

The previous chapters focused on creating your personal branding story and spreading the word about your brand. Now it's time to look in the mirror to consider how others see you.

This chapter is all about making a good first impression, whether it's with a potential client or with a future employer. We discuss the importance of appearances and manners, as well as what your body language conveys. In addition, we give you some tips for how to be the perfect host when you throw parties or sponsor events.

Keeping Up Appearances

Your personal branding story says a lot about the person you want to be. But for your brand to be authentic, you need to look the part. Keep in mind that you never know who is around the next corner, who may be riding in the elevator with you, or who will become your next most important client. It's imperative to look and act your best when you're in public.

For example, Sherry was once stepping out of an elevator with the publisher of *Midwest Restaurant News* while attending a meeting in Las Vegas. When the elevator doors opened, they nearly bumped into Dave Thomas, the founder of Wendy's International, who was there for an entirely different meeting. The publisher seized the opportunity to stretch out her hand and greet Mr. Thomas with a smile on her face, despite her astonishment.

Who knows when an impromptu meeting will lead to a long-term business affiliation? Always be prepared.

The Importance of Grooming

No matter what the career field in which you aspire, keeping up your appearance is important to your brand.

Certainly, the talent you have for a given field will elevate you among your competition. But, as many successful personalities will admit, at some point characteristics apart from talent have determined their success.

Look around at other people who have excelled in the fields in which you are branding yourself. Take notes about their style, how they wear their hair, how they dress. Take cues from those who are already successful in the field you're interested in and you will learn a lot.

Generally, follow these guidelines when you choose clothing that reflects your personal brand:

For women:

- ◆ Slacks should fit well, or be altered to fit.
- ◆ Generally, skirt lengths should be below the knee.

- Avoid cleavage-baring shirts and blouses for business settings.
- Choose simple accessories.
- Select shoes appropriate for the situation.
- Hair should be clean and well groomed.

For men:

- Purchase pants that fit well, or have them altered.
- Shirts should be clean, well-pressed, and unfrayed at the collar and sleeves. (We're aware that some brands now produce purposely frayed clothing. Save those styles for weekends.)
- Tuck shirts in unless they're styled to be worn on the outside.
- Wear a tie if it's appropriate to the situation.
- Wear a belt that matches your shoes.
- Shoes should be clean and unscuffed.
- Hair should be clean and well groomed.

Manners: The Good, the Bad, and the Despicable

Having bad manners will reflect negatively on your personal brand.

Too often people violate one of the most common of courtesies: failing to listen attentively when someone else is speaking. Looking at your watch, interrupting, or reading your text messages while someone else is talking is just plain rude. Whether you are in a job interview, in a meeting with co-workers, or simply sitting with a friend at the local coffee shop, listening to the person who is talking with you, asking questions, and providing responses are considered basic good manners.

 Tips

The firmness of your handshake and the way you look someone in the eyes may lead to your next great deal.

Dine in Style

You will have the opportunity to form many business associations during a meal or at a cocktail reception. Although good dining etiquette won't seal any deals for you, poor dining etiquette can be a deal breaker.

> **Tips**
>
> When dining at a nicer restaurant, keep in mind that your silverware will reflect the order of the meal. Your salad fork will be the farthest fork to your left; your dinner fork is generally larger and closer to your plate. Your spoons and knife will be to your right, with the larger spoon being a soup spoon. Your dessert silverware will be at the top of your plate. Beverage glasses are to the top, right of your plate, and your bread plate will be to your top left.
>
> When you are seated at your table, lift your napkin and place it on your lap once the last person has arrived at the table. At the end of the meal, place your soiled napkin, folded, to the left of your plate.

If you are invited to join a potential employer or a client during a meal and are unfamiliar with the proper manners for such an affair, borrow a book about manners from the library. It's better to be overly prepared than underprepared.

At a business reception, make it your goal to network. After all, you don't want your personal brand to say that you overload your small plate with meatballs and shrimp cocktail. Or that you have a drinking problem.

Follow these basic rules:

◆ If tables are not provided, do not try to carry too much at one time. You may want to eat a small plate of appetizers before getting a drink from the bar. Or vice versa. If you're attempting to juggle both a plate and a glass of wine, there is a greater chance that you may drop one or the other.

◆ Most cocktail receptions provide finger-friendly food. Avoid appetizers that look too messy, too large, or too uncomfortable to eat in a social situation. Use the toothpicks that are provided. Even though we expect caterers to provide proper food, sometimes they become overzealous. Use your own best judgment when filling your plate. Carrot sticks and cheese cubes are good, easy-to-eat appetizers.

◆ Drinking too much will most likely reflect poorly on you. Do this experiment: order a soda the next time you're in such a business social setting and observe the barmongers who drink too much during the affair. What kind of impression do they make?

The Importance of Saying Thank You

If you've just had a job interview, met a potential client during a cocktail reception, or received an unexpected business lead, be sure to say thank you. You can do this with a follow-up note, a quick e-mail, or a telephone call.

If you've been invited to a party, take a small gift for the host or hostess to show that you appreciate their time and their invitation. Following the event, send a note or an e-mail or make a call to let them know that you had a great time.

Taking the time to say "thank you" will reward you in many ways in the future. Make it a habit for the rest of your life.

The Ever-Important Follow-Up

Keep in touch with former professors, coaches, business associates, PTA moms, and others who have been important to your life. This small effort will assist you as you build your brand.

Your personal brand should revolve around authentic interactions with important people in your life. These relationships go to the core of who you are or who you wish to be. Periodically, drop a card or send an e-mail to check in with long-time associates. Send a thank-you note if they provided a job reference. Use the postcards you created as part of your branding collateral in Chapter 6 to let them know what's new in your life.

As your professional life continues to evolve, so will your personal and business relationships. Create a system to keep track of people, send notes, and follow up with them. You may decide to devote an hour every Saturday for this type of correspondence. Invite both old and new associates to parties and other events if they fit in. Plan lunches. Fill your professional calendar. Expand your social network. It will help you build your personal brand.

Personal Interactions via Your Body Language

In Chapter 4, we talked about verbal cues and how they affect your personal brand. Those are spoken or written words that communicate to your target audience. However, there is a lot that goes on during nonverbal communication that says a lot about you, whether you realize it or not. Understanding the basic tenets of nonverbal communication will help you be more direct in your personal communications.

The Handshake

A firm handshake will tell associates that you mean business. Upon meeting someone for the first time, or greeting him or her on subsequent meetings, grasp the person's hand firmly and look into his or her eyes as you say hello.

How you shake someone's hand says a lot about you. If you can duplicate the firmness you feel in the other person's handshake, you will be affirming that you both are equals during the conversation. But if you find the person's handshake is somewhat limp, it's okay to keep yours firm.

Eye Contact

Eye contact is another small, but extremely meaningful, type of body language that can say a lot about you and your intentions. You should always look into someone's eyes when you meet him. Also, maintain eye contact throughout a conversation to demonstrate that you are paying close attention to what is being said.

Generally, your eyes should always be focused on your counterpart's face as she is speaking to you, or as you are speaking to her. Any variance of this stance can be interpreted negatively. For example, dropping your eyes to a person's chest or legs may convey that you are not focusing on what the other person is saying. Similarly, looking around the room might unintentionally convey that you are bored.

If more than one person is involved in the conversation, you should make eye contact with everyone involved when you are speaking so that they all feel as though they are included in the conversation.

Tips

Keep in mind that your eyes will often give you away. Generally, people's eyes are wider and larger if they are really interested in the person they're talking to.

Standing Stance

The way you stand—and sit—will also convey nonverbal cues to the person with whom you are talking. Positioning your body so that you are directly facing the person you're talking with will tell them that you are paying close attention to the conversation. If you're sitting, your knees and your feet should point toward the other person to portray interest in what they're saying. If your knees and feet are pointed in an opposite direction, your position can indicate that you are not interested in the conversation.

Folding your arms as you talk with someone may mean that you have erected a barrier to what he is saying. (It may also mean that the room is too cold, though.) Keeping your arms unfolded is a better signal that you are accepting information.

Leaning toward the person you are talking with will further demonstrate that you are engaged in what is being said.

Hosting and Sponsoring Events

As you build your personal brand, you will want to begin recognizing opportunities to entertain people who are in your target audience. These situations can involve taking them to lunch, hosting a dinner party, or inviting them to an event that you or your company is sponsoring.

Are You a Mingler?

Consider the business cocktail reception that was mentioned earlier in this chapter. When you attend such an event, are you comfortable introducing yourself (with a smile and a firm handshake) to people you do not know? Do you know how to have a brief, meaningful conversation and then move on to another acquaintance?

Mingling and talking with various people during a social event—whether it's in your own home or somewhere else—is an art form that requires practice. You can practice mingling at a church social, a party that includes a dozen good friends, or during any number of informal gatherings.

Many people are not comfortable in such social settings, especially those in which they do not know a lot of others in attendance. They tend to stick with a friend or two and never move out of one corner of the room. You can quickly become the most popular person in the room by rotating around with a smile on your face, greeting others, and briefly chatting with each. You'll find that many people are delighted to meet you if you take the time to greet them. You may also find people along the way who fit squarely into your target audience.

Rules to Being a Great Host

Hosting an event can involve inviting people into your home or holding an event at a local restaurant that has private facilities for a group. Or you can sponsor an event—for a local charity or sports team—that provides you with an opportunity to entertain people by inviting them to attend a formal gala or sharing your box seats at a sporting event.

Whatever your situation, you should be acquainted with some basic hosting rules:

Plan ahead. Consider your event, who you will include, and the food and décor. Since you are hosting the event and may not always be available to converse with everyone, be sure to include another person or two on your invitation list who will keep conversation flowing when you're busy pouring drinks or taking dessert out of the oven.

Issue a written invitation at least two to four weeks prior to the event. Formal invitations should still be sent via snail mail, although invitations to casual events may be sent via e-mail or even special computer programs, such as Evite. Be sure to include the date, time, and specifics regarding what the event will include.

Be clear regarding the date your guests should respond to you regarding their attendance. Especially in the case where you have a limited number of tickets available—such as a formal gala or a sporting event—you will want to allow enough time to offer the seats to others if your first choices are unavailable. (Many folks keep a few friends in mind who may be free for that evening, in case business associates are unable to commit.)

Be clear who is invited. Are you inviting only the recipient, or are you inviting the recipient and his or her family. Or have you invited a single person to bring a guest?

Provide plenty of food and drink for those attending. Rest assured that all of your guests will be grateful if you offer a selection of snacks, if not a full meal.

Greet your guests as they arrive and express your appreciation for their attendance. Depending on the degree of formality (or informality), you'll want to invite your guests to help themselves to food and drinks.

Introduce guests to each other. Unless your group involves only intimate friends, your guests will be grateful to get acquainted with others who are attending.

Plan the order of the event. Will the food be put out before guests arrive? Will you serve dessert later? Do you have games, music, or other entertainment planned? If so, when should they occur?

Have you added surprises? Will there be a special guest? Is the dessert a special treat that will need an introduction of its own?

When your event is over, your job is to graciously walk each guest to the door, helping them get their coats along the way. Express your appreciation for their attendance, and be sure that they have not had too much to drink and that they're capable of getting themselves home. (You may need to strongly encourage guests to spend the night or to have someone else drive them home if they appear to be intoxicated.) Suggest a follow-up luncheon, coffee, e-mail, etc. Be clear that you want to stay in touch.

What Does Event Sponsorship Mean?

As you build your personal brand, it may behoove you to be an event sponsor. Such events range from charity golf outings to entire football seasons, from specific symphony concerts to nonprofit fundraising galas for health- or education-related organizations.

In return for your sponsorship, you will be allotted—depending on your financial commitment—a certain number of tickets to an event or events, an advertisement or listing in the event program, mention in pre-event publicity, and other such perks. In some cases, it may even allow you a platform during which you have a chance to address the crowd.

Choose events that will enhance your brand by getting your name out among key people in your target audience. If you are a health-care provider, for example, you may want to consider becoming a sponsor for a gala that benefits a local hospital. Most events have more than one sponsor, and most have various levels of sponsorship. You don't need to start out by being the top sponsor who contributes thousands of dollars. If you are a small business owner, you might want to make a $250 contribution in exchange for a listing in the evening's program.

Tips

Keep in mind that event sponsorship generally also offers tax perks. Consult with your accountant or tax attorney before sponsoring an event to find out how to maximize your contribution.

Your Presence and Availability

You want to be perceived as an accountable person, as someone who meets all of his or her obligations. To do so, you may be required to attend certain events, key luncheons, specific meetings, and appointments. Keep an open mind about such events; at times it may mean rearranging your social calendar—or perhaps even a vacation—to be sure that you're available when a function occurs.

If this event is a meeting, give the person conducting the meeting 100 percent of your attention. This will enhance your image. Avoid taking your laptop to the meeting, unless it is required to take notes, or text messaging during the event. Allow your voice mail to pick up your cell messages. Be engaged in the moment. Pay close attention to the person conducting the meeting and the rewards will continue to come your way.

Tips

Once you have committed to attend, don't cancel at the last minute unless there is a real emergency. Arrive on time and don't overstay your welcome.

The Least You Need to Know

- Your physical appearance should reflect the professionalism of your personal brand.

- Make it a habit to use good manners. Always.

- Be aware of your nonverbal cues.

- Practicing good social skills when you're attending or hosting an event will build your brand.

Part 3

Branding in a Modern World

Now you have the essential tools to build your personal brand and start communicating your message. But it's time to ratchet up the sophistication level of your communications strategy by exploring today's traditional and new media, as well as advertising and public relations techniques.

The capabilities currently available via the World Wide Web and various technical applications have made it easier, and at the same time more challenging, to brand yourself. You can quickly be branded by Facebook, MySpace, YouTube, a website, or blog postings without even intending to be. Branding in such an open source world requires constant management so that your message stays on target with your personal branding statement.

Chapter 9

Mainstream Media Still Counts

In This Chapter

- ◆ Demystifying the media
- ◆ Using print and broadcast media
- ◆ Becoming a personal branding media machine
- ◆ Preparing for a media interview

The media is a powerful tool to inform people about your brand—unless, of course, the words "found guilty" are linked with your name in a newspaper headline!

Media exposure can be invaluable. Getting your name "out there" creates credibility. It helps separate you from the crowd. One lawyer we know got the case of his life—tracking down the killer of a teenage boy—because the mother of the victim liked how he handled himself on television. It didn't matter to her that he was actually a zoning attorney, with no experience in criminal law. She insisted that he be involved, so he helped her work with investigators and police detectives to solve the case. In the end, he got even more media attention for his role.

That's an unusual example, but makes the point that media exposure can lead you to unexpected experiences.

This chapter focuses on how you can use the traditional media to build your personal brand. You will learn the fundamentals of becoming a one-person media machine.

A Few Examples

Here are examples of professionals who have learned to enhance their brand—or build a new one—through exposure in publications or by appearing on TV and radio programs:

- A divorce attorney and his son, a lawyer who also practices in the same field, host a weekly radio program. They offer advice to callers about domestic legal issues.

- A human resources executive gives job-hunting tips and anecdotes about her personal experiences in a column she writes for a weekly business newspaper in a large city.

- A horticulturalist with a good sense of humor and a gift of gab is a popular source for reporters writing stories about gardening. One day he got an offer to write a gardening column for the daily newspaper. That exposure led to a regular spot on a news program with a local television station.

- A high school history teacher, who is a former navy officer, writes a regular column about his two careers for a weekly paper in his small town.

- A political science professor at a large university in a major metropolitan area channeled his passion for food (and his talent as a cook) into writing by becoming a restaurant critic for a city magazine. His reviews earned him regular invitations to appear on a public radio talk show to discuss the region's culinary scene.

Demystifying the Media

Think about all the media you consume in a day. The news operations that cover your community are most likely not the same as the press organizations you turn to for national and international news. The daily newspaper on Hilton Head Island, South Carolina, covers far different topics than *The Wall Street Journal*. A TV station in Des Moines, Iowa, focuses on local issues, leaving the bigger national stories to CBS News and CNN. A city magazine in Portland, Oregon, is different from national magazines such as *Newsweek* and *Vanity Fair*.

What Is Print Media?

Print media includes print editions of newspapers, magazines, trade journals, newsletters, and so on.

Stories for print tend to be more in-depth than those in the broadcast media (TV and radio). Reporters call on multiple sources for information. Even short stories can be longer than the time TV and radio reporters have for their pieces. There also is more information overall in a print publication. It's been said that a typical TV news broadcast, if converted into text, wouldn't fill the front page of a newspaper.

Here's a rundown of the kinds of print media out there:

Daily newspapers: A daily is published every day. The Sunday edition is the showcase piece of the week. It's normally the largest paper, with more sections and longer stories. Dailies usually include a mix of international, national, regional, state, and local news.

Weekly newspapers: These papers are published once a week. Their coverage area is usually more local than a daily. They focus on a specific village, suburb, or even neighborhood in a big city. Weeklies tend to have smaller staffs than dailies. Unlike dailies, you rarely will find national or international news in a weekly. It mostly covers the events, such as the minor crimes or notices for potluck dinners, that dailies ignore.

Magazines: There are few general-interest magazines published anymore. Many have narrow niches, from women's health to skateboarding and video games to coastal living. Perhaps the most relevant magazines for building a personal brand in your hometown are city and regional publications. These magazines focus exclusively on local content, from long, in-depth articles on important issues to extensive calendar listings and lifestyle coverage.

Alternative newspapers: These are weeklies with a lot of attitude. They are more like magazines because they include long stories about local issues. But some alternative papers are less objective—that is, they have a point of view or advocate for a particular issue. They are often geared toward a younger audience and include plenty of entertainment news and listings, concentrating on music and movies.

Business publications: Some larger cities have a weekly paper and/or a monthly magazine concentrating just on business issues for that region. The weeklies write about breaking news, but have a section for promotions, awards, and other honors. Business magazines usually tackle bigger issues and profile CEOs or rising business men and women.

Trade publications: These focus exclusively on a specific industry. And almost every industry has a periodical for its members, from agriculture (*Corn & Soybean Digest*) and mechanical systems (*Contracting Business*) to metalworking (*Modern Machine Shop*) and roller rink operators (*The Rinksider*).

As you build your personal brand, consider the editors at these publications as part of your target audience.

Get to know the reporters and editors who cover your field. Collect names, titles, the name of the media outlets, and contact information. Add any short description about how that media member likes to operate or personality traits—or specialties he or she covers within your field.

> **Tips**
>
> If a journalist you work with gets a promotion or new job, send a note of congratulations. It most likely will be appreciated.

> **Warning**
>
> Try to keep your list of media contacts up-to-date. It looks unprofessional to send a media release to a person who no longer works for that publication or TV station. And it is even more unprofessional if the name is misspelled or the title is incorrect.

What Is Broadcast Media?

TV newscasts are driven by video. Stories that would be buried deep in a newspaper might lead the TV news because of great visuals. TV reporters don't have a lot of time to do in-depth reporting. Their mission is to cover what is going on right now and then move on to the next story.

Broadcast journalists have frequent deadlines, too, since there are multiple news programs throughout the day.

Working with the Media to Build a Brand

You have many options to explore in trying to become a personal branding media machine. Write columns for the paper. Become a source for a reporter. Get on the radio by hosting your own show, or even buying time to do so. Appear as a guest on a local program. Even write a book.

None of this is easy, but it's not as difficult as it may appear. The more you know (and respect) how the media works, the better your chances of making it an integral part of your branding strategy. In short, working with the media can enhance your brand.

 Warning

Treating reporters with respect won't hurt you. Treating them poorly might, however. If you are evasive or disrespectful, reporters begin to wonder what you have to hide and might start digging around.

Publicize Your Achievements

Let's look at print as an example of how to build a brand. For starters, let's think about how you can generate some media attention about an award you won. Don't just bask in the glow of praise from your friends, family, and jealous co-workers. Spread the word. To paraphrase the butler in the Dudley Moore movie *Arthur*: alert the media.

Where do you send your notice? Recall the list of print publications we discussed earlier in the chapter. Getting exposure in the daily will get you the biggest play. But it's also the hardest nut to crack. The weekly, which most likely has a smaller circulation, is still important because it is widely and deeply read (studies consistently show that the more local the news, the higher the readership). And business publications will be interested in the notice about your award.

Don't forget about trade journals that cover your industry. Also send information to your college alumni magazine or even church newsletter.

If you just won an honor for selling a lot of real estate, you can send a press release to the Homes section or the Homes writer. (See Chapter 10 for tips on good public relations techniques, such as writing effective media releases.)

Become a Source

Reporters need people to talk to for information—people they trust who can give them informed opinions and tips. If you are an expert in your field, getting quoted in the paper on topics gives you visibility, which leads to credibility. Find the reporters who cover the topic you know about and send a note saying you read their work (make sure you do), explaining that you think it's important for people to understand the topic, and offering your help.

Your goal is become like a guy in Columbus, Ohio, who does studies for developers on retail trends. He is at the top of many reporters' source lists on development/retail stories because he's accessible, reliable, knowledgeable, and humorous. He also has a knack for giving good quotes (concise, informative, sometimes clever). That's a lot of free media space for him—which leads to more business.

> **Tips**
>
> A reporter will trust you more if you don't come off looking as if you're only promoting yourself. Call reporters when you have a tip for them that isn't about you.

Understanding the Source Relationship

Reporters aren't looking to be your friend, although some may act that way. You aren't trying to be their friend, either. You should realize that the story comes first, not personal relationships. Some day you might read unflattering information about *you* over your morning coffee. That's part of the deal. If you are a great source, some reporters may try to protect you, not wanting to alienate you for short-term gain. Don't expect favorable treatment, though.

There is a thin line between being a good source and being a publicity hound. Reporters like the former and ridicule the latter. You have to be available, but not too eager. Don't call too often. Don't promote stories only about yourself. Be professional, not pushy. Give useful tips, such as a piece of breaking news that hasn't been reported yet.

Don't ever try to tell a reporter how to write a story. If a writer got something wrong, let him or her know (don't go over their heads to an editor unless the reporter isn't responsive). Most reporters want to get the facts straight and will appreciate the correction.

Tips

Some sources like to feed information to reporters, but not be named in the story. This is called "off the record." There are two kinds of off the record: a reporter can use the information, but won't identify you as the source (such as, "A city official said …"). The other is for background only. That means the source will share the information for the reporter's knowledge, but it can't be printed unless it is confirmed by another source—or as the basis for asking questions of other sources.

Make sure to confirm what kind of off-the-record information is being discussed. Trust is the key: that the reporter will keep his or her word and that you will give credible information.

Interview Tips

When talking with reporters, be concise, accurate, and informative. If you don't know the answer to a question, be honest. At the end of the interview, sum up your major points so the reporter is clear on what information you want to convey.

Being concise is even more important when working with TV or radio reporters. Your answers need to be short and crisp. You have about 20 seconds, although your actual quote might not be more than 5 seconds or so.

The best advice is to be yourself. And know what you want to say. Don't try to impress the reporter by coming on too strong, or trying to be funny.

Write a Regular Column

Becoming a regular columnist for a major daily paper requires a lot of experience and a lot of luck. Your chances increase if you have a specialty, such as legal advice, gardening, or parenting tips. You also have to be a good writer with something interesting to say.

Your chances also are better if you approach a weekly or small daily. Also think about trade journals and the local business press. Advice columns on your particular industry are always in demand with trade publications.

Write a Book

One part of the media world we haven't discussed is the book publishing industry. Yes, we know, writing a book takes time and talent. A lot of time. It's not easy to find a publisher and it's costly to publish yourself. But a book is a powerful marketing tool. People respect authors. Books create an opportunity to build credibility.

So how do you go about getting a book published? The traditional way is to find an agent. Check directories for agents who work with authors in your field. Most likely they will want to see a book proposal. The agent will either accept or reject it, or send it back for revisions.

Or you could publish the book yourself. There are plenty of vanity presses that will print it for you for a cost. Or you could go to some smaller presses that will take a chance on unknown authors.

Become a Broadcast Star

Instead of being a source for TV or print reporters, how about running your own show? Think about hosting a TV or radio program.

The opportunities for TV are limited, although cable access shows can be an easy way to start. Radio might be a better bet, particularly if you have an expertise in a field that will appeal to a broad audience. Politics, legal advice, and health care are popular topics, as well as knowledge about local restaurants. The best way to get your own show is by building a relationship with a station as a source or guest.

Hire Outside Help

If you're serious about making a media splash, you might consider hiring a media consultant who works with people, especially executives, on how to deal with the media. These experts coach people on how to work with reporters, how to be interviewed, how to control one's message, and even what to wear; and they also provide clients with inside information on how the press operates.

You also can hire a freelance publicist who will circulate your name with the media by sending press releases with your photo and a short description of your skills. You'll pay at least $75 an hour for such services, and if you hire a public relations firm, the cost will be even more. However, being associated with a public relations firm might add credibility to your brand.

The Least You Need to Know

- Ignoring the mainstream media limits your brand-building options.
- Understand your own media market.
- Building relationships with reporters can help you build your personal brand.
- Think about writing regular columns in a newspaper or hosting your own radio or TV show.

10

Understanding Public Relations

In This Chapter

- ◆ Understanding the goals of good public relations
- ◆ Posing for a professional photograph
- ◆ Creating a media kit
- ◆ PR possibilities via the web
- ◆ Creating a public relations plan

As you go about branding yourself, it is helpful to understand the public relations process. Professional PR executives know how to *frame* a brand message and how to entice the public to adopt that message. Your branding story, which you wrote in Chapter 2, will help you establish your personal public relations needs. The goal of good public relations is to gain exposure in the media— in magazines, newspapers, online websites, radio, and television.

Research has shown that nearly half of what appears in the media is initiated by public relations professionals. This is not a complex process. Good public relations can be as simple as composing a brief news release and e-mailing it to a few editors and news producers.

In this chapter, you will gain the tools necessary to put together a media kit that will show your personal brand in a professional manner. It will also explain various media possibilities that will help your brand gain exposure. Finally, it will assist you in putting together all of the pieces of public relations to create a thoughtful and reasonable public relations plan for your personal brand.

What Is Good PR?

Public relations is a four-part process that involves research, planning, communication, and evaluation of the message you have communicated. The goal of any public relations professional is to communicate a planned message.

Framing Your Message

How you frame your message to the media will determine whether it gets put into play. A media release focuses on the news. Editors and news producers at newspapers, radio and television stations, and online sites are always looking for interesting angles. You can help them do their job by providing an angle that gives them a reason to talk or write about something they may not ordinarily mention. For example, a news story focusing on English tea traditions may never be mentioned in the local news media, if no one comes forward to say, "I know about these traditions because I'm from England. And now I own a bakery where we serve English tea and scones."

Tips

When writing press releases, accuracy is paramount. Triple-check every fact, including names, addresses, and statistics.

Framing a message is often referred to as spinning a message. How you present your message will have a lot to do with whether your message is put into play by the media.

Be sure you do your research, check your facts, and communicate your message clearly. Avoid using common adjectives when you write a media release. These include words such as "wonderful," "spectacular," "delicious," "extraordinary," and "fantastic."

The Diffusion Theory of PR

The *diffusion theory* in public relations says that a person goes through five steps before adopting a message that he or she reads or hears. Those five steps include …

- ◆ Awareness: When a person first learns of a brand.

- ◆ Interest: When that person attempts to get more information about the brand or product.

- ◆ Trial: When the person samples the brand.

- ◆ Evaluation: When, after the trial, the person is determining whether he or she likes the brand.

- ◆ Adoption: When a person decides that he or she likes the brand.

For you to get someone to adopt your personal brand, you may find that you have to nurture your target audience through the first four steps of the diffusion theory. But if your target determines that he or she will adopt your brand—either by buying your services or hiring you—the early bonding that occurred during this process will work in your favor.

Entertaining the Hierarchy of Needs

Another important theory in public relations is that a target audience has a *hierarchy of needs*. Those needs are …

- ◆ Physiological: including air, water, food, clothing, shelter, rest, and health.

- ◆ Safety: protection from harm.

- ◆ Social: acceptance by others.

◆ Ego: self-esteem and self-confidence.

◆ Self-fulfillment: a need to grow to one's full potential.

When you write media releases and media advisories, you may want to consider if your brand is appealing to people in terms of any of their basic or higher needs. If so, be sure to work that information into your message. Perhaps your brand will appeal to one or more needs in this list. For example, President George W. Bush and others in his administration and on his campaign staff used Americans' need to feel safe as a public relations spin during his 2004 campaign for reelection. It worked: he got the job again.

Tools of the Trade

Good public relations means that you know which tools to use to accelerate your personal brand. There are several ways you can communicate a message to the public.

Media Releases

By releasing information to the mainstream media or publications affiliated with trade associations, it is possible to gain more exposure for your brand. Media releases are generally 200 to 500 words of double-spaced type focusing on a single, specific event regarding you or your company. A media release should be written in the inverted pyramid style. That means the primary news should be stated first, followed by the details. Your first paragraph, called the lead, should include pertinent information to the news, such as who, what, when, where, why, and sometimes how. The remaining paragraphs should fill in background information.

```
FOR IMMEDIATE RELEASE    CONTACT: Sherry Paprocki
                                  PaprockiLtd@cs.com
                                  (614) 537-7100
```

Local Editor Wins National Award

Central Ohio writer and editor, Sherry Beck Paprocki, is part of a team that has received a 2008 national gold award presented by the Council for Advancement and Support of Education.

Paprocki served as the editor for the redesign of *Marietta Magazine,* a publication for Marietta College alumni. The magazine's redesign was selected over 51 other publications in the Magazine Publishing Improvement Division. *The Stanford Lawyer* magazine, based at Stanford Law School, received the grand gold award.

Paprocki is the president of Paprocki Ltd., a publications and media relations firm based in Granville, Ohio, and located online at www.PaprockiLtd.com.

-- END --

Formatting a media release is fairly easy. The top of your page, to the left, should say FOR IMMEDIATE RELEASE (in all caps). To the right, you should write your name and contact information. Most media releases also feature a succinct headline that sums up information in the release.

To make the best impression, consider the following points when writing your media release:

◆ Professionalism: Editors like working with sources who provide professional and well-written information.

◆ Timeliness: Editors want news that is current.

◆ Accuracy: Provide correct names, dates, and other facts.

◆ Uniqueness: Publication writers and editors look for unusual angles. A media release that stresses the uniqueness of a person or a company may result in a larger feature article that is written by someone on the publication staff.

It is acceptable to submit your media release via e-mail or snail mail. If the news organization is interested in your story, they will be in touch with additional questions. If they are not interested, you probably won't get any response.

Media Advisories

A media advisory or media alert announces an upcoming event that the media may want to cover. An advisory is shorter than a media release. It is set up in a similar manner to a media release, but it has the words MEDIA ADVISORY in the upper left corner. It provides contact information in the upper right corner, a headline, and a paragraph of introductory text. The body of media advisory highlights the who, what, when, where, and why.

Here's a simple media advisory for someone announcing his or her candidacy for the local city council.

MEDIA ADVISORY   **Contact: Jake McKim**

(614) 555-1000

vote4jake@gmail.com

Local Business Owner Launches Campaign

Jake McKim, the long-time owner of the Quick Stop Lunch Spot in Westerville, plans to announce his candidacy for city council this Saturday.

Who: Jake McKim, owner of the Quick Stop Lunch Spot in Westerville.

What: Will announce his candidacy for Westerville City Council.

When: 2 p.m. Saturday, Jan. 17, 2009

Where: At the Quick Stop Lunch Spot, 2428 Central College Road, Westerville.

Why: Because Westerville needs responsible citizens to stand up and participate in its city government.

Don't overuse media advisories. Use them a few times each year, at the most, as you extend your personal brand into the community. The news media likes to stay alert to potential story ideas and news that is occurring in the community, but some people get overzealous in their attempts to work with the media. If you don't have anything new to say, don't bother saying anything.

Letters and Opinion Columns

Another route to getting published in the local newspapers is to write a letter to the editor or a longer opinion column expressing your feelings about a particular topic.

Keep your emotions tempered when you are writing a letter to the editor. The letter should be succinct and provide factual information. In your opening paragraph, identify the subject that you will write about.

In the second paragraph, talk about whether you agree or disagree with the topic you are addressing. The remaining paragraphs should include facts, examples, and statistics that support your viewpoint. Provide your name, title, organization, and telephone number at the end of your letter.

> **Warning**
>
> At all costs, avoid insulting or attacking any individuals or organization in your letter to the editor. Such strategies will backfire on you.

Generally, opinion columns—also referred to as op-ed columns—should be no longer than 750 words. Letters to the editor should be a maximum of 200 to 250 words. Choose the format that best fits what you would like to say. Most publications will require you to sign your name and provide a telephone number. They will not publish the telephone number, but someone at the paper might actually call you to confirm information that you have written.

For instance, if you're a Realtor, you might want to write an opinion column about the sluggishness of the real estate market and why that may be a benefit instead of a hindrance. You might encourage potential buyers to purchase a home while there is a large selection available on the market. This type of column will encourage readers to see a silver lining in an otherwise dreary market. What do you get out of it? Free publicity.

Publicity Photos

If you find yourself continuously digging through a heap of pictures or an electronic file of snapshots for a decent photo of yourself, then consider getting a professional headshot to keep on file for publicity purposes.

Many professional photographers will shoot a good, well-lighted headshot for a nominal fee—sometimes starting as low as $50. Call a local professional photographer and ask what he or she would charge for a publicity photo. This will provide a basic photograph for a variety of situations, including the following:

- An announcement in local newspapers and professional trade publications regarding a job promotion, new business, appointment to a board, or a special award.

- The release of a book or to promote book signings.

- Advertisements in publications and trade journals.

- Use on various marketing collateral, ranging from postcards to billboards.

Once you schedule an appointment for a publicity photo, make sure you look the part:

- Choose a suit or an outfit that won't be outdated within a few years. Even though this is just a headshot, your upper torso will appear in the photo. You want your publicity photo to be good for the next five years.

- Choose flattering colors. Most publicity photos are shot in color, but can also be reproduced in black and white.

- Wear simple jewelry.

- Once you are in the studio, relax and enjoy the process. A good, professional photographer is usually adept at helping you smile and look relaxed in the final photo.

Media Kits

A media kit is similar to a marketing packet. It is distributed to the media to provide background information about a person, product, or service.

As you develop your personal brand, there may be occasions in which a media kit will be helpful. You can often use the same folder you use for your marketing kits, but you may want to include some additional items in the packet that goes to the media.

Here are some items you may want to include in your media kit:

♦ A bio that includes your professional history and any outstanding awards and honors you have earned.

♦ A resumé, if applicable.

♦ A professional publicity photo.

♦ Any professional articles that have been published about you or your business.

♦ Media releases regarding you and your business. These can be written by you or someone else that you pay to help you.

Be selective about what you put in your media kit . Provide no more than 6 to 10 pages of information. Also, be sure to include your business card, either by stapling it in a conspicuous place on your folder, or by inserting it into a slot specifically designated for it.

Creating a Public Relations Plan

Now that we have examined a wide range of ways that you can use public relations tools as you build your personal brand, consider creating an official *public relations plan*. What will you send to the media and when will you send it?

def•i•ni•tion

A **public relations plan** is a blueprint of what you want to do and how you will accomplish the task. A good plan should include a timeline for media releases, media advisories, advertising, and other promotions. It should also include a budget.

If planned properly, you might be able to generate several media hits from a single event. Consider this example.

We know a woman who left her job as a fashion designer and started to bake English treats to sell at the local farmers' market. She is considering opening a full-fledged bakery in the future, so exposure in the community media is important.

Instead of writing one news release about her new business for the local newspapers and television stations, she could consider releasing information three different times to the local media.

Scheduling releases three different times may provide her with more exposure in the community. Her initial public relations plan may simply look like this:

- ◆ October 1: Media release announcing new business and the products that customers can order.

- ◆ November 15: Media release focusing on her native English heritage and holiday traditions. This release may result in a larger feature during the holiday seasons that will spin an international perspective.

- ◆ January 15: Media release focusing on the traditional English tea party and the morsels that can be purchased from the new bakery.

Also, she will want to consider whether she will be participating in any events that would require a media advisory. Finally, she may want to look at the online possibilities for marketing her baked goods. Chapter 11 will look at brand building via the web in more detail.

The Least You Need to Know

- ◆ Public relations involves working through traditional and online media to communicate a message.

- ◆ Take the time to carefully frame your message in such a way as to capture people's attention.

- ◆ Any materials that you submit to the media should be well-written, using proper grammar and punctuation.

- ◆ A media kit should provide background information about your brand for editors and producers.

- ◆ A public relations plan helps you organize your efforts to build your brand through the media.

11

Branding Yourself Via the Web

In This Chapter

- ◆ Promoting your brand on the web
- ◆ Designing your personal website
- ◆ Making the most of social networking sites
- ◆ The pros and cons of branding on the web

Your personal brand can get a big boost from the World Wide Web. And the web's role in branding will only grow in the coming years. Thanks to the web, people no longer simply sit back and absorb the culture; instead, they create it, shape it, and critique it.

People now collaborate in ways that were unimaginable only a few years ago. They create vast networks, solve complex problems, and exchange ideas with colleagues from around the globe.

To build a personal brand, today it is important that you engage on the web. But simply participating in the web culture is not enough; you must also be true to your brand.

This chapter explores the vast range of popular online tools available for building your personal brand, from building your personal website to creating a vlog.

First, though, let's consider the story of a woman named Julia Allison who has built her brand using the many tools available on the web.

A Personal Branding Story

After graduating from Georgetown in 2004 with a degree in political science, Julia decided that she wanted to be a writer. She moved to New York and got a job as a weekly columnist for *Time Out New York*. Four years later, Julia had created pages on MySpace and Facebook, accounts on Twitter and Flickr, four *blogs* on Tumblr, three blogs on Movable Type, as well as videos on Vimeo and YouTube. Of course, she also had a personal website.

On the blogosphere, Julia Allison became a star. As she continued to build her brand online, she landed some writing gigs for *Maxim*, *Cosmopolitan*, and a few other print publications. Once the mainstream media got wind of her popularity on the web, she landed appearances on TV, eventually making more than 350 appearances on shows such as *Access Hollywood* and CBS's *Early Show*. She became such a huge web phenomena that *Wired* magazine ran a picture of her on its cover. Why? Because of her web savvy.

def•i•ni•tion

The term **blog** comes from the word *weblog,* which was created by an American named Jorn Barger in 1997. The term was shortened to blog in 1999. A blog is a website usually devoted to a particular topic. For instance, someone with a passion about growing hostas in eastern Virginia wants to share his knowledge on that topic. He can establish a blog and start writing about his expertise. Blog content can range from text to video. The person writing the blog is a called a **blogger.** The act of adding to a blog is **blogging.** The entries on a blog are called **blog posts.** Blogs can range from a person writing about what they ate for breakfast to a highly credentialed lawyer explaining the intricacies of the federal sentencing guidelines. You can set up a blog through various websites, such as Google, Facebook, and many others. **Blogosphere** is the term coined to describe the greater community involving all blogs.

Some people groan when they hear Julia Allison's name. She has done such a good job of promoting herself that she seems to be everywhere. But her success at promoting herself on the web is something that everyone can learn from.

Websites

As you begin building your brand on the web, the first thing you should consider is whether you need a personal website. (If you already have a website, be sure that it's up-to-date.)

A website provides a prime opportunity to explain what you do and why you do it better than your competitors. Here are some examples of people who have used websites to promote their personal brands:

- A coastal Realtor uses his website to promote his history in the area, as well as his expertise in selling property on an isolated island.

- A southern California attorney uses his website to promote his specialty in bankruptcy law.

- An OBGYN uses her website to emphasize her expertise in fertility issues.

- An Arizona writer/speaker uses her website to promote her book about bicycling.

- A Washington, D.C., plumber uses his website to promote his services in the area.

> **Warning**
>
> Our web-savvy culture even has a name for fake blogs: flogs. You'll get hammered for trying to fake who you are and what your motive is.

Having a personal website will also tell your business associates that you are web savvy.

To Get Help, or Not

There are several ways you can go about building your own website. The easiest, of course, is to have a designer or a web guru build it for you. If you have more time than money, the best way to design the website is to do it yourself. You may be able to do this by using preformatted templates offered by a company that also provides you with e-mail, such as Google Sites or Yahoo! Site Builder.

Once you have a site, you will need to register a domain name and assign a site host for it. Two companies that can help you with those tasks are GoDaddy.com and hostmonster.com. Keep in mind that there is usually a small fee for registering a domain name and contracting with a host.

A California writer named Kathy has used her website to promote her expertise on health and parenting topics. She uses her home page to describe her background, the awards she has received for her writing, and the top publications where her byline has appeared. This is all summarized in only three paragraphs. Her photo appears on the site as well.

The tabs on her home page give readers access to a complete list of publications, a list of speaking engagements, a variety of her published clips, and quotes from editors who have worked with her. All of this information helps build Kathy's credibility among editors looking to hire her.

Like Kathy, your website should break down your achievements into small, bite-size portions. If you are a visual artist, for example, you will probably want to include a page that shows pictures of your work.

Tracking Visitors

Once your site is up and running, you're going to want to make sure people know about it. Be sure to list your website on all of your public relations materials, including your business card and all media releases.

def•i•ni•tion

Search engine optimization is the process of improving the volume of traffic on a website.

Search engine optimization experts can help you attract visitors as well. Optimization experts use specific keywords on websites and specific HTML phrases that encourage more website traffic. Once your website is drawing traffic, you can attempt to collect data from website visitors so that you have a way of getting in touch with future clients.

Take a lesson from President Barack Obama's campaign website, which drew a lot of traffic during the 2008 primary and general election. Obama's technical advisors were experts at gathering information from the website's visitors. When someone registered as an Obama supporter, he or she filled in a form with her e-mail address and telephone numbers. Obama's campaign organizers created databases from that information and then were able to send regular e-mails and text messages to Obama's supporters. Even on the evening that Obama was elected president, his campaign office sent a quick "thank you" in a text message.

Real World Brands

During the 2007 lead-up to the Super Bowl, Frito-Lay sponsored a contest in which it encouraged viewers to submit a 30-second Doritos commercial. Five winners would be selected to attend the Super Bowl and, in the end, two commercials would be aired. Frito-Lay was able to track visitors to its website. In the first week, the website received 2 million visitors and 50 submissions. Before the contest was over, about 1,700 videos had been submitted. Frito-Lay did an excellent job leading television viewers to its website.

Electronic Newsletters

Electronic newsletters are well-designed e-mails sent to a list of recipients. They are especially useful if you already have experience in a certain career field and you wish to present yourself as an expert, or a consultant, in your field. They work well for authors, art dealers, insurance agents, real estate brokers, and others who want to keep in touch with their target audience.

Programs such as Constant Contact help you create pre-formatted newsletters. Such programs are easy to use and

 Tips

Electronic newsletters and your business cards are two ways to drive your target audience to your website. Be sure to register your domain for your personal website before you print your business cards.

relatively inexpensive. In addition, these services offer basic tracking options so you can find out which recipients actually opened the e-mail. You may find the small fee for any of these services well worth the expense.

> **Warning**
>
> If you decide to create an electronic newsletter, be sure that it looks professional. You can avoid some embarrassing mistakes by asking one or two other people to proofread it before you release it.

E-mail Blasts

If you are attempting to put out a small bit of information that helps to promote your personal brand, then you will want to consider a simple e-mail blast. Unlike an e-newsletter, an e-mail blast usually only deals with one topic. It can serve as a quick alert to your audience. Here are some ways people have successfully used e-mail blasts:

◆ A local farmer sent a "final harvest" notice to his regular customers inviting them to show up at 10 A.M. on Saturday for all the free produce they could carry away. He explained that the first frost was due to arrive any day and remaining fruit and vegetables would die on the vine if not harvested before then.

◆ An artist announced his art opening at a local gallery the following week.

◆ A travel agent blasted a note to frequent customers informing them of a great last-minute deal on a Caribbean cruise.

Podcasts

Podcasting allows you to become your own radio or TV talk show host. You, too, can be like Oprah. But instead of appearing on radio or TV, you are creating audio or video content and distributing it over the Internet. Your podcast can be viewed and listened to on mobile devices such as cell phones and iPods as well as personal computers.

Podcasting allows you to communicate a message to your target audience and gives your audience the opportunity to see what you look like and hear how you sound.

Podcasts can range from the amateur varieties most often seen on websites such as YouTube to professional productions that some organizations use as training tools for their employees.

A book author we know did a humorous video podcast about his latest release. He staged a one-sided telephone conversation in which he talked to a friend about why Oprah had not called him to be on her show.

Other professionals can greatly benefit from doing podcasts. A chef, for example, could post an instructional video podcast on how to cook a favorite dish. An artist could post a video podcast of himself working on a new piece. Even a physician can create a podcast discussing the latest research in his or her chosen field.

> **Real World Brands**
>
> Barack Obama's 2008 campaign made frequent use of podcasts to promote Obama's brand. Campaign staff chair David Plouffe mentioned that at times he simply sat down in front of his laptop-installed video camera and started talking because he felt that he needed to communicate with Obama's followers that day

Social Networking

Public relations possibilities abound with social networking sites such as Facebook and MySpace, as they offer opportunities for virtual word-of-mouth communication.

Facebook and MySpace boast more than 100 million members each. Facebook claims that its users upload 24 million photos daily. Additional features, such as the ability to track all of your Facebook friends via their cell phone locations, are being added. Given the popularity of these sites, it only makes sense to consider adopting them as part of your branding strategy.

Facebook and MySpace

If you are not a Facebook or MySpace member, it's time to consider becoming one. At the very least, creating a member page will show your target audience that you are plugged in to the latest communication network and that you are ready to go to work. If you are already a member, take a hard look at your personal page and critique what you have there. Do the photos and verbiage reflect the best possible brand that represents you? Is it a brand that your target audience will appreciate?

First, think about how you defined your target audience back in Chapter 3. Are you trying to get a job in a field where the managers are the ages of your parents and their friends? If so, determine whether your parents and their friends would appreciate your Facebook entries. If not, why not?

If your target audience reflects your own peers, does your Facebook page fit what they would expect?

Tips

What's the difference between Facebook and MySpace? Whereas Facebook has a largely college-age audience, MySpace's members tend to be younger than college age. In addition, MySpace offers more graphic and design options.

If you are creating a business of your own, you can use Facebook to promote it. For example, consider our friend who has a small soup business called the Soup Loft. Because he lives in a college town, it behooves him to promote his business to the 3,000 college students who live within walking distance. He has set up a Facebook group for the Soup Loft. This way he can build community among some of his best customers. He also posts his menu on the Soup Loft page and updates it regularly.

LinkedIn

Unlike MySpace and Facebook, LinkedIn was created with the professional person in mind. To date, it claims a network of 25 million professionals from around the world. LinkedIn touts its ability to link you to others in your industry to make potential job and sales contacts. It's less of a chatting tool, but instead an instrument used by professionals who want to meet others who can help them. If you choose to use LinkedIn, be sure that you're taking advantage of all of its options, including its extensive member network.

You can promote your personal brand on LinkedIn by first completing your biographical information. Then, the goal is to link to anyone you know on the network.

One guy we know, who is a partner in a sports training facility, linked with everyone he knew on LinkedIn so that it would help him sell memberships to the training facility. Another person we know uses LinkedIn to connect with her friends who are in broadcast jobs all over the country.

YouTube

Founded in 2005, YouTube is a vast website to which people post video clips that anyone can access and watch. YouTube viewers number in the millions and generally range from 18 to 55 years old. Another service similar to YouTube, though with a smaller viewership, is Vimeo. Sites like YouTube and Vimeo can provide some intriguing public relations opportunities for your personal brand. All levels of people use YouTube, from small bands trying to promote their music to top corporations advertising their products and services.

You can drive traffic to your personal website by creating a video, posting it to YouTube, and then embedding it on your personal website. We know an author who did just that, to complement a book she wrote about the peace movement of the 1960s. To make her book relevant to today's readers she recorded an interview she did with an Iraq war veteran, posted it to YouTube, and linked to it from her book site.

Twitter

Twitter is one of the newest social networking sites to hit the web. It enables users to inform friends and family about their minute-by-minute activities. Twitter's website brags that you can learn more about your online acquaintances by knowing what they're doing between blog posts and e-mails. Users can release short posts (140 or fewer characters) and broadcast those messages to others via a website, instant messaging programs, or cell phone.

Why would you want to broadcast your everyday movements to hundreds or thousands of people? Twitter has the ability to be quite annoying if you alert friends to your actions on a regular basis, but don't rule it out as an important tool to promote your brand. For instance, Twitter is a useful tool if you're in the business of updating clients regarding the most effective products or services that your company has available. But you'll only have 140 characters to relay your message, so efficiency is important!

Also, we know artists and authors who use Twitter to announce their openings, releases, and publications. If you're a radio show host, you can use Twitter to send out a teaser about your upcoming program. If you're the director of an animal shelter, you could use Twitter to alert your community when you have too many cats and dogs. Twitter is a quick, easy way to blast out a brief message and see immediate results.

Blogs

With the millions of blogs already posted to the web, we encourage you to scrutinize your rationale for joining the masses and launching your own blog. Nonetheless, there are reasons that you may want to have a blog. If you're in the position of updating clients regarding products, services, and ongoing research, a blog posting may be a great way to get out your message. If you are a writer or an editor who wants to communicate more frequently with readers than your publication will allow, blogging might be a good option.

Mommy blogs have seen growing popularity in recent years, as an effective way for digitally savvy mothers of young children to stay in touch. In fact, some mommy blogs have become so popular that advertisers are signing up en masse and daddies are resigning their full-time jobs to help out at home.

Real World Brands

Heather B. Armstrong is a former graphic designer who started her blog in 2001; her site has since become one of the most well-read mommy blogs on the Internet. (Check out www.dooce.com.) She talks about her life as the mother of a preschooler on her blog that now sports advertisements from Samsung and other major corporate brands.

Vlogs

A *vlog* is a variation of a blog, combining the diary style of a blog but in a video format. A vlog is like having your own ongoing reality show.

Like blogs, you will want to really consider if having regular videos posted on a website will enhance your personal brand. It may depend on the age range of your target audience and what their expectations are for you and your brand. For example, if you are marketing your garage band on the web, a vlog may be a good way to communicate with your audience. But if you're selling mortgages, your audience probably won't expect vlog updates.

Internet Forums

Internet forums were among the first ways that people began communicating on the Internet. Generally, an Internet forum is a virtual gathering space for people who have similar interests.

Today, most professionals communicate with others of like interests on professional forums connected with specific organizations or associations.

Advantages of Using the Web

No matter what your field or your interest, to fully promote your personal brand it is essential that you have a web presence. Here are the major reasons:

- If you're launching a business, consumers expect it to have a web presence.

- Your website will help your target audience bond with you. It will provide others with a depth of knowledge about your personal background that should make them more comfortable with you.

Tips

Starting a new business but haven't had time to build a website for it yet? You can always reserve your domain name and put up an "under construction" sign on a temporary web page.

◆ Your target audience may try to investigate you beyond the information you have provided them. If they don't find anything about you on the web, they may worry that you're not digitally savvy.

Pitfalls of the Online World

We are in a period of radical readjustment, not only in the ways we communicate, but also in the ways we use our time. Online networking has become more popular, but experts are saying that we're losing the skills to network with others face-to-face, in person.

As you build your personal brand, we encourage you to be selective regarding your online presence. Use the tools that will work best to help build your brand, but don't waste time on others. Once you decide on the right tools, be vigilant about keeping them up-to-date.

Keep in mind that relating to people is about personal networking. To build your personal brand, you need to create an emotional bond with your target audience. Although the most recent web technologies can help you build your brand, it takes patience and persistence to connect with other people.

The Least You Need to Know

◆ Your personal website should reflect and expand on your resumé.

◆ Use social networking sites such as Facebook, MySpace, and LinkedIn to promote your brand.

◆ YouTube is the most popular site to post video clips.

◆ Be selective about which tools you use to promote your brand on the web, and be vigilant about keeping your information up-to-date.

Chapter 12

Personal Communication in a New Age

In This Chapter

- ◆ Using e-mail to promote your brand
- ◆ Communicating with your audience via text messaging
- ◆ Practicing good communications etiquette
- ◆ Choosing the right means of communication for your target market

In the previous few chapters, we talked a lot about branding yourself on the web. In this chapter, we want to drill deeper into the way many people brand themselves online, often without even realizing it. For instance, how you communicate with colleagues and clients via e-mail and instant messaging can have a substantial impact on how people perceive your personal brand.

In addition, this chapter addresses branding yourself via other information-age communications methods—cell phones, text messaging, messaging on social network sites such as Facebook and MySpace, and web conferencing.

We are now in an era often called *Web 2.0*, in which the web is shaped by people who use it. The use of blogs, wikis, podcasts, and social networking sites allows us to contribute to, critique, and have more control over the web's content.

Where Do You Fit In?

Are you a Baby Boomer? Or are you part of Gen X (born generally between 1965 and 1981) or Gen Y (born somewhere between 1977 and 2002), the latter also known as the Millennial generation? Once you answer that question, it will enable you to begin sorting out these various communication devices and how they fit into your personal branding strategy. For example, young people tend to communicate much more frequently via text messaging than Baby Boomers.

No matter what your age, though, we encourage you to keep an open mind about new and varied methods for communicating and to sort through the range of possibilities to determine which will be most effective at helping you build your personal brand. Your profession may also have a lot to do with how you choose to communicate your brand.

Keeping on top of technological advances is part of the challenge of branding yourself. Unless you want to be labeled old-fashioned and outdated, we advise that you keep current with the changing pace of today's communication devices.

E-mail

About 15 years ago, e-mail was the latest, greatest tool for communicating with peers and co-workers. Today, however, e-mail has lost some of its luster, particularly with young people, who opt to instead use text messaging via cell phones, instant messaging, social network messaging, and other, constantly evolving, forms of communication.

Yet there are times when e-mail is still indispensable.

Tips

The way teenagers communicate today will affect the way we all communicate in the future. In the spring of 2008, the Pew Research Center released a report that found that 36 percent of teens prefer communicating with friends via text messaging, 35 percent talk on cell phones, 35 percent talk on home phones and land lines, 29 percent use instant messaging, 23 percent send messages via a social networking site, and only 16 percent communicate via e-mail.

Even though people who are part of Gen X and Gen Y are using e-mail less often, we doubt that it will fade from glory anytime soon. First developed in the 1960s, e-mail programs predated the development of the Internet, which came in 1969. E-mail was initially used as a way to store information in a mainframe computer. Its social purposes didn't come into play until companies such as CompuServe and America Online got interested in it.

Today, e-mail has become a widely acceptable way of communicating for business and personal purposes.

As you develop your personal brand, make it a habit to check your e-mail at least once a day. If you don't check it regularly, you may well lose out on either an important social engagement or a professional career lead.

Here are some tips for putting e-mail to good use as a branding tool:

◆ Send a polite follow-up after you meet someone who has the potential to be important to your personal brand. Example: a public relations professional meets a magazine editor at a luncheon. The initial follow-up e-mail from the PR pro simply says that it was nice to meet. However, the PR person hopes to establish a bond with the editor leading to the eventual placement of an article for a client.

◆ Use e-mail blasts to announce your new products, new publications, store or gallery openings, or matters of public concern. Example: The executive director of a mental health agency sends e-mail blasts several times each year to keep taxpayers updated regarding governmental funding. This boosts her personal brand of being a reliable public employee who focuses on transparency of public funding.

◆ Use e-mail to build a following. Example: a local citizen is concerned with the decisions being made by the city's elected school board. That citizen uses e-mail to communicate decisions to friends and associates immediately after the board's monthly meetings. This citizen creates a following so that when he announces that he will run for a position on the board, he already has a committee willing to work for his campaign.

◆ Use e-mail to gather a crowd. Example: each Monday a wine shop owner sends out a simple e-newsletter about the wines that will be featured at Thursday night's tasting. This builds the owner's brand of being knowledgeable about wines as much as it builds his business.

◆ Use brief, one-on-one e-mail notes to stay in touch with major clients, potential employers, and others who are in a position to help your brand. Example: if you know that a client has given birth, had surgery, or gotten a promotion, send a quick note checking in and wishing them well. Don't expect a response; your goal is simply to let them know that you're thinking about them. This gives authenticity to your personal brand as a caring individual.

Think about these additional etiquette tips when sending e-mail:

◆ Anything you write can be forwarded to anyone else (or everyone else).

◆ Even though it's a common practice, it is unethical to forward someone else's e-mail or other written material, without getting their permission to do so. In some cases, in fact, it may be illegal.

◆ Make sure the subject line matches the body of the e-mail. If it's too vague, people might think it's junk mail.

◆ Be aware that jokes, sarcasm, and irony do not translate well in e-mail. Friends may get it, but people who don't know you very well may not.

◆ Be careful about criticism. What you write sometimes comes across a lot harsher in e-mail than intended. Reserve criticism for private face-to-face or phone meetings.

◆ Get to the point. E-mail is most effective as a concise, brief message.

◆ Don't use all capital letters. That's the equivalent of shouting at your audience.

◆ Don't be too quick to hit the send button, particularly if you are angry. Take a few minutes. Then reread and revise. You might want a trusted colleague to review it, too.

◆ Sign your message with your name and identifying information if your target audience isn't familiar with your e-mail address.

◆ Be careful to proofread. Silly mistakes can negatively affect your personal brand.

Instant Messaging

Instant messaging, also known as IM, is a real-time communication tool that allows you to correspond directly with others.

Instant messaging is primarily used for personal or social communications. However, some corporations use internal instant messaging systems for employees to communicate with each other so that they don't fill up their e-mail boxes.

You should never use IM to initially try to sell products or make contacts with new customers. But if your existing clients or customers express a preference for using IM, by all means go for it. For example, you might send an IM if you need to confirm an order your client has sent you. This can be an immediate and efficient mode of communication.

Tips

The Centers for Disease Control and Prevention reported in 2008 that one in six households in the United States had no land line and used only cell phones. The CDC further reported that of adults under 30, one in three did not have a land line; of people over 65, only 2 percent did not have a land line.

Cell Phone Calls

The prolific use of cell phones requires some consideration of cell phone etiquette, too:

◆ Don't assume that cell phones can be used to make sales.

◆ Don't carry on professional conversations in public places. Example: You are a financial advisor waiting for a plane at the airport. You receive an urgent call from a big investor. Instead of engaging in a business discussion regarding the client's private affairs in a public setting, offer to return the call from a quiet spot. Furthermore, don't even bother to answer the cell phone if you are in a location that is too noisy for your caller to hear you. Pick up the message, find a quiet spot, and then return the call.

◆ Don't assume that there are no messages because you haven't heard your phone ring. Unfortunately, cell phone connections are far from perfect. You might have been out of your service area without even knowing it, and someone might have called and left you a message without the phone ever ringing.

◆ Don't expect that a business associate returning your call has listened to your message. Cell phones provide a fast "return call" feature when a person looks at the incoming number. They may choose to call you instead of listening to your message.

Warning

Just because you can use your cell phone anywhere at any time does not mean that you should. There is mounting evidence that cell phone usage leads to traffic accidents. The National Institute for Occupational Safety and Health cites inattentive driving—which includes reading, talking, using the phone, and fatigue—as the leading cause for vehicle collisions with semi-trucks.

Text Messaging

Text messaging is a convenient way to share brief, informal messages. Text messages are typically limited to 160 or fewer characters per message.

Today's technology allows text messages to be sent from your cell phone to other phones, instant messaging systems, and laptop and desktop computer e-mail. With special accessories, land line telephones can even be adapted to receive text messages.

Warning

Check with your cell phone provider to find out what kind of texting plan you have. Supplemental texting charges can be extraordinarily expensive if they aren't part of your plan.

As with any relatively new form of communication, don't assume that someone knows how to text message unless you've texted them in the past or they have given you permission to text with them.

Texting can be used to enhance your brand, as the following examples demonstrate:

- Text a client or associate if you want to quietly alert him that you're running late. Example: Your morning meeting is running long and you will be late for lunch. Texting enhances your brand because you're being accountable for your tardy actions while eliminating the need for a telephone conversation.

- If appropriate to your brand, use texting to set up meetings with regular clientele. Example: We know a personal organizer who has six digitally savvy clients. She regularly texts them regarding appointment times. This enhances her brand as being efficient, well organized, and responsive.

It is best to avoid:

- Checking text messages (and responding to them) during meetings. If an emergency occurs, politely excuse yourself from the meeting immediately upon getting the initial text so that you can respond in a more private setting.

- Using text messaging to make sales. The word limit provides little opportunity for building an emotional bond if you don't already have one.

- Texting associates repeatedly if they don't respond after the first message.

Facebook's Wall Messaging and More

Social networking hardly existed five years ago. Today, however, sites such as Facebook, MySpace, Friendster, and LinkedIn offer various options for building your brand over the web.

Warning _____

A 2008 survey of 320 college admissions officers from some of the country's top colleges found that 10 percent of them look at social networking sites such as Facebook and MySpace when they're making their admission decisions. At least one college admissions officer said that his college rescinded an admissions offer to a student after finding negative information about the student on a social networking site.

Here are tips about building your brand on social networking sites:

♦ Use your page to promote a cause. Example: President Barack Obama created a Facebook page before many people even knew who he was. As his reputation grew, he used his page to promote his campaign and to rally his supporters.

♦ Create a group. Once you have created a page on a social networking site, you have the opportunity to join and create specific interest groups. Example: A local coffee shop owner creates a group named for his coffee shop. During slow times, he blasts out a message to the group online and offers special deals on coffee drinks.

♦ Ask for introductions. Example: If you notice that one of your contacts on LinkedIn or another social networking site is linked with someone who might be of value to your career, ask to be introduced. Don't assume, however, that the mutual acquaintance will respond if you ask them to link with you.

The Blogosphere

Technorati, a company that attempts to keep track of the blogs in the ever-growing blogosphere, reported in 2008 that 184 million people around the world have started blogs and 346 million people read them.

Somewhere between 60 and 94 million people in the United States read blogs. In other words, the blogosphere is changing the way Americans do business, get the news, and share information. That's one reason why Procter & Gamble decided to court the top mommy bloggers in 2008 by sending them freebies and inviting them to meet. This international corporation recognized these bloggers as important word-of-mouth contributors to the success of their brands.

If you intend to create a blog, or are already hosting a blog, be sure to make it pertinent. You have written your branding story, so you know your areas of expertise. Create your blogging niche and stick with it. Don't become another blogger who just wants to talk about themselves to see if anyone is listening.

Real World Brands

Three years ago, Kathy Sena was a regular contributor to *Woman's Day* magazine when her editors there invited her to do a dieting blog. Her blog, which lasted for three months (she lost 18 pounds), ended up getting Kathy assignments from other editors at other publications. Soon after the *Woman's Day* blog ended, she started her own blog called ParentTalkToday.com. Now, she says, she can't imagine not blogging because it has led to fresh story ideas, new friends, and a new community. Certainly, her personal brand and her bottom line have been enhanced by blogging.

Consider how your blog fits into your personal branding story. Here are some tips for using a blog to promote your brand:

- Stay focused. If you create a blog, stick to your niche. Example: A local magazine's restaurant reviewer creates a blog that talks about eating adventures across the country. This enhances his brand because he can share experiences outside the magazine's circulation area.

- Offer wisdom. Blog about things that other people need to know. Example: You are an accountant who can provide advice throughout the year, not just at tax time. This enhances your brand because you can alert your clients, and potential clients, to changes in tax laws, new write-offs, and other benefits.

- Build on bonds. Your first readers may be your immediate friends and family. But if you are offering good, pertinent advice, your readership will grow. Example: An accountant announces his blog with an e-mail blast to everyone he knows. If the advice is good, then those associates will pass along his tips to others.

- Set yourself apart from the crowd. Why should people listen to you? Know what makes your personal brand stand out and use that in your blogging advice. Example: A newspaper reporter in a small coastal town knows that there's little advice available to tourists who want the inside scoop about where to eat. He creates a blog to talk about menus and reputations of local eateries. In addition, he posts alerts when restaurants open and close, as many of the town's visitors come back each year.

Keep in mind that some blogs make money by hosting advertisers, but it takes work to make a living out of blogging. Technorati found that four out of five bloggers post brand or product reviews. More than half of all blogs post paid advertising. Some bloggers have found advertising to be extremely profitable, earning $75,000 and more a year from it.

The Wiki

A wiki is a simple page or website that allows anyone with access to contribute. Wikipedia is the best-known wiki on the web today. Developed in 1994 by Ward Cunningham, wikis are becoming more mainstream for planning, problem solving, and collaborating.

A wiki page makes it easier for all involved to update information, make assignments, view other people's reports, and perform various other tasks. Your successful coordination of a wiki project will gain you much respect from peers and clients. Here are a couple of ways that a wiki can be helpful to your personal brand:

- It allows immediate input. Example: A conference organizer establishes a wiki page so that committee members can add speakers as they are recruited. It allows the organizer to stay on top of the committee's progress, thus enhancing his personal brand as a leader. Don't make changes to entries that have been made by others in the group, however, until you have discussions with that contributor.

◆ It allows a project to evolve. Example: A group of medical professionals is collaborating on a journal article. The project coordinator is able to stay on top of the process to be sure that everyone is meeting deadlines and that the project will be completed in a timely manner. This process enhances the group leader's brand of a deadline-oriented project manager. The wiki page helps the group stay on schedule without constant inquiries about its progress.

To Skype, or Not?

Created in 2003, Skype is an international voice calling system. A quick download from www.skype.com will enable you to talk to people around the world, free of charge. Unlike earlier generations of Internet calling, Skype provides clearer communications. Skype has more than 300 million regular users, enabling easy, worldwide conversation in real time. To provide more flexibility, Skype also offers paid service to land lines and mobile phones.

The Skype computer program not only permits voice communication, it also has a real-time chat component in which you can have an online text conversation and video conferencing if you have a video camera connected to your computer.

Web Conferencing

Web conferencing is a way for people in different physical locations to have meetings online.

Tips

Some web conferences, known as videoconferences, are done with the use of video cameras so that everyone participating in the conference can see each other's faces. If you are part of a videoconference, be sure to dress in business attire even if you're a telecommuter sitting at your kitchen table. Speak clearly and look directly at the video camera on or connected to your computer when you're talking.

Web conferencing can be a great way to enhance your personal brand. When hosting a web conference, you should always stick to a schedule and follow a basic agenda that you've distributed to participants in advance.

Here are some other tips for successful web conferencing:

◆ Sign on to the required website and call the required telephone number three to five minutes before the web conference is scheduled to start. If this is your first time participating in a web conference, you may want to practice the sign on earlier.

◆ If you are late to sign on and call in, try not to disturb a web conference already in underway.

◆ Unless you are leading the call, or unless you have a lot of questions to ask, consider muting your telephone so that other conferees aren't disturbed by background noises. If you choose not to mute your phone, be sure to participate in the conference from a quiet location.

Opportunities abound for promoting your personal brand through the latest wave of new communication techniques. Some communication methods, such as text messaging, are more suitable for talking with friends. Others, such as web conferencing, are generally used in professional settings. As you develop your personal brand, stay aware of the communication trends and choose those that work best for you. Keep privacy in mind and remember that the Internet is the least private form of media that exists—anything posted online can help—or ruin—your hard-earned reputation.

The Least You Need to Know

◆ Being aware of and able to use the wide variety of new web-based communication techniques can enhance your personal brand.

◆ Social networking sites provide outlets for communicating your brand.

◆ Be polite and professional no matter what communication method you're using to promote your brand.

◆ Not all forms of communication may be appropriate for promoting your brand. Consider your communication options carefully.

Should You Buy the Mad Ad, Men?

In This Chapter

♦ Advertising your personal brand

♦ Creating an advertising plan

♦ Selecting your advertising vehicles

♦ Planning your message in advance

People sometimes confuse public relations with paid advertising. As you are now aware, the focus of public relations is to provide the media with information, using tools such as media releases that cost very little to prepare and distribute—unless, of course, you hire public relations professionals to do this work for you.

Advertising, on the other hand, always has a price tag. That price tag can vary from less than $100 for a small newspaper ad to millions of dollars for a multimedia advertising campaign.

In this chapter, we review the various channels of advertising, ranging from ads in newspapers and other publications to ads on the back of T-shirts. You'll learn when it's important to advertise and how advertising may be helpful as you build your personal brand. Finally, we discuss how you choose the most effective advertising vehicles and create a plan that you can put into action.

Why Should You Advertise?

Advertising is a way to persuade customers to purchase your product or service. It can be one of the most expensive line items for an entrepreneur or business owner.

If you're promoting a new brand, advertising will expose it to a target audience. Later, advertising will strengthen the emotional bond with your target. The entire goal of advertising is to gain and retain customers. To do so, you should strategically think about your needs.

A good advertising plan, also sometimes called a *media strategy*, will force you to examine your budget. You should familiarize yourself with various modes of advertising, the expenses involved, and the demographics they target. After you do that, you will have the background needed to form a basic advertising plan.

When Should You Advertise Your Personal Brand?

Brand loyalty, of course, should result in sales. If a company's advertisements create a consistent look and feel for a brand, then the brand becomes more recognizable to its target audience. In the end, of course, advertisers hope to obtain brand loyalty, which will lead viewers to regularly purchase their products or services.

Here are some suggestions of ways that various types of professionals may want to advertise:

◆ A small-town family physician will want to advertise within a specific geographic region. Therefore, the best choice may be to advertise in the community's newspaper or on the community's website. Professional practitioners generally avoid advertising on billboards and on television.

♦ A city-based plastic surgeon will want to advertise to a high-end demographic. Therefore, she may want to advertise in upscale city magazines that have affluent readers who live in her region. An advertising sales rep can help the surgeon sort through the frequency, size, and pricing options.

♦ A Realtor is usually focused on selling homes in a specific territory. That Realtor can choose from print publications and broadcast stations in that region. An advertising plan will probably involve entering a contract with the local publication, perhaps advertising on the local television station and—if funds are available—adding some extras such as billboards and such.

♦ An entrepreneur opening a gelato store will probably have a very limited advertising budget. Buying a small advertisement in a well-read publication may be all it takes to get customers. Sometimes hanging a sign works just as well.

Whether you are a medical professional, retailer, real estate broker, insurance salesperson, or recent college graduate looking for a full-time job, your personal needs for advertising will vary widely. Before you decide your advertising plan, first learn about the range of advertising channels available so that you are considering the full scope. Ask questions regarding the potential audience for an ad, the age and gender of the audience, and other pertinent facts.

If you don't ask questions, your advertising dollars can be easily misused. For example, just because someone is selling banner ads on a new website intended for people on the market for a new home, it doesn't mean that every Realtor in town is going to jump on board the site. Buying an advertisement on the website won't do you any good unless the site actually gets traffic from potential buyers. Advertising before the website owner can prove that he or she has a large following of potential buyers might be a waste of your money.

Most ad representatives get a percentage of what they earn, so they should be happy to spend time communicating with you regarding your advertising needs, if they believe that you will contribute to their income in the coming months. Any ad sales representative should provide you with the following information:

- Audience numbers: How many readers or viewers will see the ad?

- Advertising packages: What sizes, periods of time, and numbers of ads are available?

- Prices: Every advertisement has a price, but today's ad packages may include web services, print, broadcast, and other package mixes.

- Demographic information: Specifics regarding the gender, age, income, and other valuable information that would impact your brand.

Tips

Demographics are important. For example, if you're advertising a math camp for elementary-age children, you don't want to advertise on a radio station with a demographic that involves mainly teenagers. Instead, you may want to search for a radio station that targets parents during their morning drive time.

Types of Advertising

The many ways that you can advertise are referred to as *advertising channels*. The size of your target audience, the type of your personal brand, and the extent of your advertising budget will determine when and where you should advertise. The following sections describe a variety of possibilities.

Broadcast

Advertising in broadcast means buying commercial spots on radio and television.

Tips

Arbitron (www.arbitron.com) is a company that looks closely at radio stations, their audiences, and their popularity. This company can help you determine which stations get the largest audiences in your area. Nielsen (www.nielsenmedia.com) will do the same for television, although its services will cost you money.

You should try to stretch your advertising dollars as far as possible by advertising with the station or stations that have the largest number of viewers or listeners within your target audience. Generally, ads purchased in the broadcast media will be broken down into seconds and minutes. If your budget allows, 30 seconds of airtime during primetime programming, Monday through Friday, is long enough to make an impact with your target audience. When you advertise with the broadcast media, be sure that the time of day—or night—your ads appear will hit your target audience.

Car dealers, Realtors, retailers, and others can benefit from the visuals that television offers. Personal brands that don't depend heavily on visuals should buy more radio advertising. They may include political candidates, musical groups who have scheduled performances, lawyers who want to promote their area of expertise, and those in similar professions.

Webcasts

A webcast is streaming video that appears online. A webcast can be created with a specific product or service in mind and used as an advertising vehicle. Many websites can host advertisements in the form of webcasts. Some websites you may want to consider advertising on include local newspapers and television stations, websites focused at specific niches of people who would want to buy your products or services, and popular sites such as YouTube, which has an extensive advertising and partnership program in place.

If you own an insurance business or investment company, for example, you can build your brand by paying for a webcast on a website owned by a local television station or newspaper. A webcast offers the opportunity to introduce yourself to your audience and encourages them to buy products from you. Unlike a broadcast commercial, which only airs during scheduled times, a webcast can be viewed online anytime someone clicks on it.

A webcast might be particularly useful if your personal brand involves performing. Whether you are a musician, a vocalist, or a magician, a webcast that shows you in action can increase bookings and boost name recognition.

Real World Brands

YouTube claims to have the sixth largest audience of viewers on the web, with 68 million users each month. That's important to national corporations that want to spend advertising dollars on the website. But it can also be important to you. Many start-up musicians, bands, and other performers upload YouTube videos for free to get initial exposure for their brands. YouTube provides a viable international market place for advertising. Keep YouTube in mind if its viewers fit your target audience.

Before you get too excited about producing an advertisement via webcast, find the right niche that targets your audience. Then determine whether webcast advertising fits into your budget.

Websites and Blogs

The website for your local Chamber of Commerce may reach 200 or more people each week. The website for your professional organization may reach its entire membership. As you put together your advertising strategy for your personal brand, determine whether a website or blog can get you the most bang for your buck. Some websites may offer the opportunity for webcasting, as previously discussed, whereas others will only offer static advertisements similar to those used by the print media.

Tips

Consumers are willing to spend more time watching commercials on TV than on the web, according to a Cabletelevision Advertising Bureau survey. For example, while 24 percent of respondents said they would watch a 45- to 60-second commercial on television, only 8 percent would view one of that length online.

Watch out for websites and blogs that exist for the sole goal of selling advertisements. Of course, the more popular a website or blog, the higher its ad rates. For example, advertising on Facebook and MySpace today will be much more expensive than it was when the two most popular social networking sites were just starting. If you're wondering how popular a certain website is, consider using Google's page ranking system and www.prchecker.info; it can help you determine how many hits the website gets.

Here are ways people can promote their personal brand through website or blog advertising:

◆ An entrepreneurial sandwich shop owner decides to advertise on the local college's website by offering a coupon to students, faculty, and other employees.

◆ An accountant advertises his services on the local Chamber of Commerce website since the community's small businesses are Chamber members and potential clients.

◆ A tutor places an advertisement on the website of the local school district in an attempt to build her name recognition and her business.

◆ A coffee shop owner opens a special play group for toddlers (and their moms) and decides to advertise on a blog produced by a well-connected mother in the community.

◆ A college student establishing a brand as a graphic designer advertises on another student's well-read blog. He's attempting to build his brand (and his portfolio) by designing graduation invitations for other students.

Newspapers and Magazines

Well-established print publications can have readerships that range from a couple hundred for weekly community newspapers to several million for national magazines and newspapers. Generally, advertising in a local publication is going to be less expensive than advertising in a publication that has a national distribution.

Print publications will give you ad specs that will tell you exactly how much an ad will cost. Rates will vary depending on the size and frequency of the advertisement, as well as whether it will be in color or black and white.

Personal brands that are confined to specific geographic regions usually benefit the most from advertising in print publications. Those brands usually involve insurance and investment brokers, physicians of all specialties, dentists, Realtors, car dealers, and other such professionals who want to bring in new business on a regular basis.

The Telephone Book

Buying a business listing or another advertisement in the local telephone directory is an especially smart move if you have a product or a service that is locally focused. Ads in a telephone book may work best if you have a service that people need immediately such as plumbing, heating and air conditioning, or electrical work. Generally, a listing or a larger advertisement will be good for a year in a publication that is well used in every household. If your area is covered by more than one telephone directory, find out which is the most popular before placing an ad.

Tips

As younger generations snub the local telephone companies in favor of cell phones, their households may not receive a telephone directory. But don't be hasty in cutting the phone book out of your ad budget. Gen X and Gen Y may use online directories that are also created by your telephone company. For example, AT&T, which provides printed yellow pages, also operates yellowpages.com online. When buying an ad, be sure that it will appear in both locations.

Direct Mail

Direct mail advertising may work well if you're attempting to promote your brand within certain zip codes. You can purchase mailing lists from companies that create such lists or you can obtain them from other places, such as voter registration lists from your county government office.

With the ever-increasing cost of postage, direct mail is more expensive than it used to be. To keep costs down, consider mailing an average-size post card, which is the most cost-efficient size. And be sure to follow *bulk mail* procedures established by the U.S. Postal Service to get the best possible rate. You can find more information about mailing and postage rates at your local post office or at www.usps.com.

Political candidates, especially, benefit from such bulk-mailing campaigns. For others who want to blanket a certain territory, such as retailers and artists having openings or special sales, bulk mailing is also an option.

Personal Letter

If you're just starting a business or looking for a job, you may want to send a handwritten note to your closest associates informing them of the news and asking for their support. In today's high-tech world, a handwritten letter is one of the most authentic ways to promote your personal brand.

Endorsements and Sponsorships

Opportunities abound for spreading the word about your brand through endorsements and sponsorships.

Endorsements and sponsorships can start for as little as $100 and run into the thousands and millions. Sponsor a Little League team and the youngsters will wear your name on the back of their shirts all season long. Endorse a local charity event, and your name will probably appear in advertisements, news stories, catalogs, and brochures.

 Tips

Endorsements and sponsorships may have tax benefits if you're dealing with official nonprofit organizations. Check with your accountant to find out more about these tax advantages.

Warning

Don't be too fast to turn away someone seeking an endorsement or sponsorship in your community. The goodwill that you buy with potential clients and customers may go a long way to building your personal brand.

Buttons and Bumper Stickers

Sometimes buttons and bumper stickers can say a lot about a brand. If you're planning to run for political office, certainly, check out this advertising option. An ice cream shop is another brand that can benefit from handing out bumper stickers to its customers. Even orthodontists can benefit from the bumper sticker option, since parents spend many hours driving their children around.

Posters

Posters placed in neighborhood grocery stores, diners, and coffee shops can have a positive effect on your personal brand, if they're designed and used in a professional manner. Realtors who wish to advertise a specific home may put a poster in the local coffee shops. Authors may want to use posters to promote readings at the local libraries. A seamstress starting a new business can easily advertise with an inexpensive poster placed on bulletin boards around the neighborhood. Other service professionals can also benefit from a well-designed and well-paced poster.

T-shirts and Other Apparel

Putting your name on a T-shirt can generate a lot of attention for your brand.

How many times have you stopped to read a T-shirt that someone is wearing or that is hanging in a store window? Names on T-shirts and other apparel can be great conversation starters. It could be the beginning of a whole word-of-mouth marketing campaign that costs you nothing at all after you've paid for the shirts.

When considering advertising on T-shirts or other apparel, think carefully about the number of items you will need. Do you need a variety of sizes? Can you get away with printing on an inexpensive T-shirt, or do you need a higher-quality item? Also, keep in mind that most companies will charge you a one-time set-up fee to create the artwork or wording necessary for your clothing in addition to the fee for the apparel.

Airplane Banners, Billboards, and More

One of the more unique ways to advertise your personal brand would be to hire an airplane to fly your banner over a football game or a rock concert. Though this is a rather unorthodox and expensive way to advertise, don't rule it out. The time and place may be just right for advertising your personal brand over a stadium filled with people.

And if your brand involves running a local business, the most effective way to reach a potential customer day after day may be to have a large photograph of yourself smiling down from a billboard on the highway.

There are dozens of other unorthodox ways to advertise today—have your name or mug put on pizza boxes, on double-decker buses, taxis, commuter trains, and more. There seems to be an endless number of places where you can post your personal brand.

Devising an Advertising Plan

If you have decided that your personal brand can benefit from advertising, talk to sales representatives about the various advertising vehicles you're interested in. You'll need to get the details of each to determine where you will put your money.

It helps to begin each year with an advertising budget. Design a simple monthly plan to follow so that you stay within your budget and get the most impact from your advertising dollars. The more you know about your advertising vehicle, the smarter you will be when spending ad dollars.

Be sure that any advertisements you place are professionally created and convey the appropriate message about your brand. Continuously strive for a cohesive brand identity to enhance your personal image.

 Warning

Avoid giving in to pressure from sales representatives to purchase unbudgeted advertising. Doing so will throw off your advertising budget. Instead, stick with your advertising plan.

The Least You Need to Know

- Advertising is a way to persuade people to purchase a product or service.

- There are many ways to advertise, beyond print publications, broadcast stations, and online sites.

- If you are approached to advertise online, be sure to get audience numbers that convince you that the website is viable.

- Create professional advertisements that reflect your brand identity.

Chapter

14

Guerrilla Tactics in a Noisy World

In This Chapter

- ◆ Building your brand with guerrilla marketing
- ◆ Why guerrilla marketing is more than just outrageous stunts
- ◆ Making guerrilla marketing cost-effective
- ◆ Avoiding guerrilla marketing mistakes

The practice of getting people's attention through marketing is not limited to the Nikes and Coca-Colas of the world. Marketing can be an effective branding strategy for small businesses and solo operators. And one of the most effective marketing strategies for individuals is guerrilla marketing. The beauty of guerrilla marketing is that it doesn't have to cost a lot of money.

In previous chapters, we have written a lot about using different tools—from traditional media to the web and advertising to public relations—to build your brand. In this chapter, we discuss how those same tools can be employed in a guerrilla marketing campaign.

Guerrilla marketing is a great way to capture people's attention in a noisy market.

What Is Guerrilla Marketing?

Guerrilla marketing is an unconventional way of spreading the word about yourself or your product. It originally was viewed as a means for small businesses to effectively market themselves inexpensively. A classic example is the rock band that distributes homemade fliers instead of buying advertising space. We also are aware of a tax-preparation business with a patriotic name that attracts business by hiring a person dressed in a Statue of Liberty costume to hand out brochures.

Guerrilla marketing has evolved to include the use of outrageous stunts and behavior. Big corporations now employ guerrilla marketing tactics, too.

def•i•ni•tion

Guerrilla marketing is an unconventional way of spreading the word about yourself or your product. The term is credited to Jay Conrad Levinson, who is considered to be the father of guerrilla marketing. He has written a series of books on the topic, starting with *Guerrilla Marketing* in 1983. He has since sold more than 14 million books around the world. Levinson also is the chairman of Guerrilla Marketing International. He says guerrilla marketing is less about the money you invest than it is the time, energy, imagination, and information.

A Few Definitions

Guerrilla marketing also is known as extreme marketing, grassroots marketing, or feet-on-the-street marketing. Some subsets of guerrilla marketing are as follows:

- **Viral marketing** involves getting users to forward your message (for free) through e-mail, blog postings, and so on.

- **People's marketing** is about getting your customers involved in marketing you or your product. For instance, a car dealer could ask customers to send photos of themselves with the cars they bought at the lot to be posted online and at the business.

◆ A **wild posting campaign** is a way to spread the word about you or your product through posters, decals, or other temporary means. For instance, many organizations on college campuses advertise upcoming events by writing chalk messages on campus sidewalks.

◆ **Buzz marketing** promotes a product without the audience knowing that it's actually being marketed to. For example, you could get people you know to go to a bar to mingle and talk about you or your product as if they were holding a normal conversation. This is also known as undercover marketing or stealth marketing.

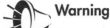

Warning

The practice of buzz marketing is deceptive. If people find out that you engage in it, you could damage your brand.

Building a Guerrilla Marketing Campaign

Before you run out to rent a chicken suit to wear on the street corner, here are some things to consider:

◆ Figure out your story. How can you solve someone else's problem? How can you be the solution?

◆ Where do you fit in the market? This is determining your niche or position.

◆ Pinpoint your target audiences: the people who need what you are selling.

◆ Set your goals.

◆ Do your research.

◆ Brainstorm creative ideas.

◆ Set a budget.

◆ Once you figure out a plan, commit to it. Repetition is important in building brand awareness.

◆ Be patient. Getting results takes time and depends on building relationships.

- Maintain the plan.

- Be consistent with your message.

Tips _____

Research shows that marketing represents at least 4 percent of a company's budget.

When it comes to a guerrilla marketing campaign, smaller is usually better. As a small business or individual, you can be nimble and aggressive. You don't have to run ideas past a bunch of committees and wait for approval. Guerrilla marketing is about being efficient.

Do Your Research

In trying to spread the word about your personal brand, you'll want to do research on your target audiences.

Who is your target audience?

Trying to answer that question might sound expensive. But you don't have to hire pollsters or survey firms. You can do your own research. A lot of information is available for you to tap into yourself.

There's the Internet, of course. (We have addressed how to build your brand through the web in Chapters 11 and 12.)

And remember that thing called a library? People there are trained to help you for free. They think finding information is fun. Ask them for help.

Ask your customers questions, too. What do they want? Why do they buy from you?

Your local chamber of commerce is a source, as well as trade associations. Information on marketing also can be found at the American Marketing Association (www.ama.org).

And contact sales reps for newspapers, magazines, or broadcast stations and ask for a media kit, which will include valuable demographic information about your market.

Be Creative

The more you know, the more creative you can be. It's like building a fence. If you have a small pile of wood, you'll have a small fence and might even have to use a few bad pieces of wood. But the more wood you accumulate, the bigger your fence, and the better it will be because you can toss out the bad pieces.

Warning

Creativity doesn't always mean clever advertising or a catchy slogan. It's how you do business: the way you interact with people or even your choice of where to locate your business.

Creativity has to be on target, too. We all have seen funny commercials, but can't remember the name of the company or the product. What's the point? If a creative campaign doesn't fulfill its purpose, then it's not successful.

To run an effective marketing campaign, you must stay on top of current events. You need to know what's going on, not just in your industry, but in the world in general. Be knowledgeable about current affairs, trends, pop culture. You can feed off what's happening right now, staying on top of trends and new ideas. You never want to look as if you are out of the loop.

Tips

One tactic to draw positive attention is to offer freebies. Who doesn't like getting something for free? We're not talking about trinkets, but useful information. If you are a real estate agent, hold a free seminar for first-time homebuyers, for instance. The key is to build a relationship. And it never hurts to offer free food, such as coffee and doughnuts.

Don't Stop Marketing After the Launch

Advocates of guerrilla marketing say that you can't stop once you start. They say once you put a plan in place, follow the plan and keep doing it. Repetition is key. If you stop, people will forget you. Also, people move all the time. You will always have a new audience to persuade.

And don't think your message is so memorable that it is lodged in people's brains like an annoying song. If some people can't remember their wedding anniversaries, why should they recall your business pitch? Keep the messages coming. By continuing to market, you don't allow the competition to get an edge. If you stop, you're wasting an investment and losing your place in the hearts and minds of your customers.

Marketing is a process. It has to be part of building your personal brand. Once you put a plan in place and take action, you can't coast. You have to remain vigilant.

Building Partnerships

Is there someone with whom you can share marketing expenses? We know a dentist who gives free exams to a restaurant owner in exchange for free lunches. They also each do referrals for the other.

If you are a financial planner and want to send a newsletter to clients, you can broaden your reach by partnering with your competition: other financial planners. Together, you can reach a much wider audience. You'll be offering clients a broader range of services, and the partnership helps to reduce your expenses.

Word of Mouth

Perhaps the most powerful guerrilla marketing campaign is word of mouth. You want people to say good things about you, so you need to give them a positive experience.

The feel-good experience can be as simple as making sure you smile and remain upbeat. Or it can be as elaborate as some of the tactics used by Howard Dean's 2004 Democratic presidential campaign.

Although he ultimately failed to win his party's nomination, Dean made a remarkable splash on the national scene. His surge was created in part by word of mouth: his supporters held gatherings in their homes to watch a video of him explaining his campaign. Those guests went to work the next day and said good things about Dean to their friends. The process was replicated throughout the country. It created buzz that didn't cost a lot of money.

How can you achieve the same results? Ask someone you have worked with to put in writing the specific benefits he or she received from you. This will serve as a powerful testimonial about your products or services. Think about how we make product choices or even hire people. If people we know and trust say they believe in a thing or person, we look favorably on that recommendation.

> ### Real World Brands
>
> In the 1980s, Rollen Stewart attended sporting events wearing a rainbow-colored Afro wig. He would position himself in the stands so he could be seen on TV, such as in the end zone near the goalposts at NFL games. Then he would stand and hold up a simple sign that read "John 3:16." For relatively little cost, he got millions of people to read the biblical message.

A Few Examples

To help generate ideas for your own guerrilla marketing campaign, it helps to read about what others have done. The following sections outline some guerrilla tactics that have been used by individuals, small businesses, and corporations.

Living the 1960s

One woman we know wrote a book about where some key 1960s radicals ended up decades later. She promotes her book by holding readings. Sounds conventional enough. Except she dresses as if she were still living in the era. Her appearance sends an effective visual message about the book and helps build her brand as an expert on that decade.

Yo-Yo Mama

Maria Carilao founded Yobonic Yo-Yos in Seattle in 1997. Working with a low budget, she developed creative ways to market her product. She went to the FAO Schwarz store in New York City and tied yo-yos to the doors and attached her business cards to get the store's attention. She also covered her Volvo with colorful yo-yos and called herself the CEyO of the company.

She got a lot of press during the scandal involving President Clinton and Monica Lewinsky by producing a Presidential Blo-Yo.

T-Shirt Exposure

A couple of years ago, the marketing director for QVC challenged company employees to help promote the brand by incorporating the business's T-shirt into a guerrilla marketing campaign. The winner would get $10,000. Ideas ranged from a worker recruiting eight other people to wear the T-shirts while skydiving and forming the letter "Q" during the jump. Some employees posted a video on YouTube. The winner managed to get a T-shirt prominently displayed on the Jay Leno show.

Million-Dollar Bra

Victoria's Secret is a $5 billion a year business. It has a huge marketing budget. But one of its most successful campaigns was rooted in guerrilla marketing: a supermodel posing in a multimillion-dollar bra studded with diamonds the company promoted during the holidays. The stunt built brand awareness even though 99.9 percent of its customers would never buy one. The stunt generated a ton of press attention that reinforced the sexy, upscale nature of Victoria's Secret's brand.

Derrie-Air

The *Philadelphia Inquirer*, the *Philadelphia Daily News*, and Philly.com combined to create a fake ad campaign featuring an airline called Derrie-Air, which based the cost of a ticket on a passenger's weight. The idea was to cause an uproar to prove that people still pay attention to print ads.

Biking in Place

In Melbourne, Australia, an Australian news network set up a promotion on a busy sidewalk to draw attention to its coverage of the Tour de France in 2008. A man dressed in bicycling gear rode a stationary bike that powered a scrolling billboard.

Taking It to the Streets

Amnesty International protested the United States government's policy of holding detainees at its facility in Guantanamo Bay, Cuba, by putting a cell replicating the ones used at the prison on a sidewalk and inviting people to sit inside.

Pop-up Businesses

The jeans manufacturer Levi's has opened temporary retail outlets inside other stores. A young owner of a clothing store set up a portable stand on a sidewalk of a busy city street to sell her wares. After selling one item, she would move the stand to a different street—and also update her location on her website.

Tips

The idea of temporary kiosks in both retail and non-retail environments appears to be a growing trend.

Staging Events

In Chapter 11, we wrote about how Julia Allison built a brand through her expert use of new media tools (she's the one who became famous for being famous, an online version of Paris Hilton).

Allison also knows how to employ guerrilla marketing tactics. One day in 2008 in New York, she and a handful of friends went to Times Square dressed as Jazzercise instructors and danced around on the sidewalk. A large crowd gathered to watch while a couple of cameramen brought along by Allison documented the event, which she then posted on her website.

Guerrilla Marketing and the Law

Be careful that your guerrilla marketing campaign doesn't cross the legal line. In Chicago in early 2007, a young man riding a Chicago Transit Authority train was caught placing stickers on the train wall.

The stickers promoted a video game. It turned out that a marketing firm doing work for the video game manufacturer had paid the man $100 to put up the stickers. He was actually breaking the law by defacing public property. A marketing rep was quoted as saying he was aware of the law, but the practice helped to sell videos and associated the brand with being cool and underground. Most guerrilla marketers emphasize that laws should not be broken when employing a campaign.

> **Tips**
>
> There's an old marketing saying that it takes at least seven impressions before people begin to remember your message.

A Guerrilla Marketing Campaign Gone Awry

Guerrilla marketing can backfire, causing a negative reaction. Take a famous recent case in Boston.

In early 2007, 400 light display boxes were set up in 10 cities to promote a late-night TV program, *Aqua Teen Hunger Force*, on Turner Broadcasting System's Cartoon Network. The small device featured a character from the show extending a middle finger. There was no explanation.

The light displays didn't cause any trouble—except in Boston. Authorities were alerted about a possible explosive. Main streets were shut down and numerous public safety agencies were mobilized. The city spent about $500,000 before it realized the device was an act of guerrilla marketing by a New York agency hired by Turner. The incident caused an angry reaction and sparked national attention.

On one hand, it can be argued that the campaign was effective. A lot of people heard about the TV show because of the press coverage. According to media reports, its ratings went up by 5 percent the week after the event and activity on the Cartoon Network's website more than doubled.

On the other hand, Turner paid a $2 million fine and issued an apology. The brand was associated with causing a public panic.

Another Tactic Gone Bad

Dr. Pepper's guerrilla marketing promotion in Boston sounded like a good idea on paper: it was a treasure hunt in which contestants would follow clues to find a hidden coin. The person who found the coin would win $10,000.

The coin, however, was hidden in a cemetery that holds the remains of such esteemed American patriots as Paul Revere and Samuel Adams, as well as members of Benjamin Franklin's family. When city officials learned about the stunt, they called it disrespectful and potentially harmful to the grounds. A Dr. Pepper spokesman ended up apologizing.

The Least You Need to Know

◆ Guerrilla marketing is about using creativity instead of money to promote your brand.

◆ Effective marketing plans must be maintained after the launch.

◆ Finding low-cost ways to gain attention can have a big impact.

◆ Word of mouth is perhaps the most effective tool of a guerrilla marketer.

◆ You can be outrageous, but respect the law.

Part 4

Brand Extension and Evolution

In this final section of the book, we look at how to extend your brand into other arenas. If you're a personal trainer, perhaps you could extend your brand by offering health and fitness seminars to local businesses. If you run a restaurant, you might consider extending your brand into catering for weddings and other events.

To help inspire you, we turn to the lessons that mega-brand personalities such as Ellen DeGeneres, Donald Trump, Tiger Woods, and Oprah Winfrey can teach us.

Chapter 15

If You Brand It, They Will Come

In This Chapter

- ◆ Understanding brand extension
- ◆ Determining whether you're ready to extend your brand
- ◆ Extending your brand through teaching
- ◆ Considering the risks of brand extension

Brand extension is normally associated with big-name companies, which use their reputations in the marketplace to launch new products or services. However, people with well-established personal brands can do the same thing.

In this chapter, we explain brand extension, examine how it works in the marketplace, and point out how you can use the same concepts to extend your personal brand. In addition, we provide examples of how other people and companies have successfully used brand extensions.

What Is Brand Extension?

Brand extension is the process of launching new products or services based on an existing brand.

Launching new products is expensive and risky (studies say that 9 of 10 fail). By using a well-known, trustworthy brand to launch affiliated products and services, companies can cut costs—spending less on introducing the product to consumers—and increase the chances of success.

Among the examples typically cited by branding experts are two well-known cleaning products.

Ivory Soap

What comes to mind when you hear about Ivory Soap? Most likely, a hand soap that's gentle on your skin.

The maker of Ivory Soap, Procter & Gamble, extended the line of its core brand by starting Ivory Liquid Hand Soap. It's still soap, but instead of buying it as a bar, you get it as a liquid in a bottle. Same product, different delivery.

Procter & Gamble also extended Ivory Soap into a different category by starting Ivory Dish Soap. It's still a cleaning product, but instead of cleaning your hands, it cleans your dishes. The common denominator is the brand name Ivory.

Clorox

When you hear the name Clorox, you probably think of a strong, but effective, cleaning product. It might be difficult for Clorox to extend its brand into, say, hand cleaning. However, it has extended its brand into other areas that call for a tough cleaning product, such as a toilet bowl cleaner and disinfectant wipes.

Extending a Personal Brand

Celebrities seem to have good luck with extending their personal brands. Here are some samples of brand extensions by folks who are well known in their respective fields.

Jimmy Buffett

Jimmy Buffet is a great example of someone who leveraged a strong personal brand to create multiple brand extensions. Once a struggling musician, Buffett eventually hit it big. His music captured a fantasy life of hanging out by the beach with few worries and plenty of tropical refreshments—all captured in his huge hit "Margaritaville." His popularity grew, and he developed a highly loyal following of fans who bought his recordings and flocked to his concerts.

Buffett has extended his brand to restaurant chains, a line of tropical footwear, clothing, outdoor furniture, and even blenders. He even has a channel on Sirius radio devoted solely to his music.

While Buffet may sing about a lazy way of living, he's been anything but a slacker in extending his brand.

Ralph and Terry Kovel

Before his death in September 2008, Ralph Kovel—along with his wife, Terry—wrote books that became the bibles for the antique industry. In fact, they published 97 guides over more than 50 years. The first book was *Dictionary of Marks*, dealing with the markings on the bottom of porcelain and pottery. That was 1953.

They extended the brand by writing books about other antiques-related topics, as well as a syndicated newspaper column, a newsletter, and magazine articles. They even started a website and hosted a television series on PBS and Home and Garden Television.

The Kovels turned a passion for antiques (which began on their honeymoon in Bermuda) into a lucrative brand and at the same time established themselves as the authorities on pricing for antiques and collectibles.

Celebrity Chefs

You can find plenty of celebrity chefs who understand the value of brand extension. Thanks in large part to the success of the Food Network, more and more people are becoming celebrity chefs.

Julia Child was the first celebrity chef, and she extended her brand with a TV show and cookbooks. Now, chefs have extensions that go beyond broadcasting and publishing: speaking engagements, product lines, and more.

Here are three examples of people who know their way around the kitchen and how to successfully extend a brand.

Paula Deen

Based in Savannah, Georgia, Deen got her start out of desperation. In 1989, she was recently divorced and suffering from panic attacks that prevented her from leaving her home. As a way to make some money, she started an in-house business called the Bag Lady. Her two young sons delivered the lunches she made to area offices. (She soon overcame the panic attacks.) Her business grew into a catering service and then a restaurant in downtown Savannah called The Lady & Sons.

The restaurant became a huge hit and she began to extend her brand: she wrote books packed with recipes for Southern cooking and then launched a magazine. She also started three TV shows: *Paula's Home Cooking*, *Paula's Best Dishes*, and *Paula's Party* on the Food Network. And she created a line of branded food products.

All of her extensions are consistent with her brand: a colorful personality with a skill for cooking old-fashioned Southern food.

Emeril

Minus the early personal turmoil, Emeril Lagasse followed a similar path as Deen in extending his brand. Like Deen, Emeril started with a restaurant, in New Orleans, called, appropriately enough, Emeril's Restaurant. By 2008, he owned 10 restaurants.

He, too, extended his brand by authoring a number of cookbooks and hosting television shows (and became famous for his signature line, "Bam!," while cooking). He sells Emerilware, a line of kitchen products. And he has a food line: Emeril's Kicked Up Tomato Pasta Sauce, Emeril's Steak Rub, and more. You can buy an Emeril's Adult Chef Coat (with Emeril's logo). He even endorses such products as Crest toothpaste.

In February 2008, Emeril sold his operation (excluding the restaurants) to Martha Stewart Living Omnimedia for about $50 million. Not a bad payoff for extending his brand.

Real World Brands

It's hard to think of a company that is as closely linked with its founder and CEO as Virgin. Richard Branson opened a record store in 1971 in London. He built upon the success of Virgin Records to launch a record label. Then he jumped into a bunch of new categories: an airline, a cell phone company, soft drinks, cars, wines, and more. Behind it all has been Branson and his forceful personality.

Starting Points for Extending Your Personal Brand

You don't have to be a celebrity to launch an extension for your personal brand. Here are some ideas to get started:

- The owner of a small hair salon can offer other services, such as facials, waxing, and massages.

- A photojournalist can freelance as a wedding photographer.

- A deli owner can start a catering service.

- A musician can give lessons or build a recording studio.

- A nurse can accompany the tour guides during trips offered by an adventure travel company. (It would be a selling point to advertise a nurse as part of the leadership team for people traveling in exotic places.)

- A financial planner can conduct a public seminar on her area of expertise.

- A graphic designer can develop a line of greeting cards to sell at a local shop.

- A teacher can start a tutoring service.

- An IT expert can launch a side business that fixes people's home computers.

Head to the Classroom

You may be at a point in your life when you have acquired the skills necessary to teach others. For instance, both of us began teaching journalism classes as adjunct instructors at a small liberal arts college in our late 30s. Check with community colleges and liberal arts schools for teaching opportunities.

In addition to extending your brand by establishing yourself as an expert in your area, you will experience the joy of introducing others to your field.

Develop Patents, Websites, and Stores

We know a podiatrist who treats patients by offering clinical advice and, when necessary, performing surgeries. He is well respected and established in his community. But he wanted to share his knowledge and help more people. Here are a few ways he extended his brand:

◆ He created and patented foot-care products.

◆ He established a website that became a center of discussion for patients and doctors relating to podiatry. He helped people not only in his community, but throughout the country and, in some cases, in other nations.

◆ He opened a store that sold shoes known for providing proper foot support.

While his core brand is related to his work at his office and in a hospital, he extended his brand into the areas of education, product development, and retail.

Cult Brands

Ideally, you want to build a *cult brand*. A cult brand has a following that is unbelievably loyal. Consider Jimmy Buffett, whose admirers call themselves Parrotheads. Also think about the fans of Oprah Winfrey and Martha Stewart. We're talking fanatics. These brands seemingly can do no wrong. And the brand extensions of Buffett, Stewart, and Winfrey have been wildly successful.

Another example of a company with a cult brand is Apple. It's not just a computer company, but also a leader in creativity and design. That's why people camp out at its stores before they open to get the newest products, including such brand extensions as iPods or iPhones.

Deeply committed customers and fans are called *brand evangelists*. They create excellent word-of-mouth marketing for the brand and its extensions. Who wouldn't want a loyal group of evangelists promoting you or your products and services via social networks and other methods?

Think Twice Before Extending Your Brand

Brand extensions take time and thought, and they aren't suitable for everybody. Just because your brand is well known doesn't mean you should launch an extension.

Remember, it's important to stay consistent with your brand. If your brand has an upscale image, don't enter the low-rent market. Think Donald Trump. His extensions include vodka and steaks, not beer and hot dogs.

Real World Brands

Jeff Gordon is a famous NASCAR driver who has won more than 80 races in his career. His brand is almost entirely associated with racing high-performance automobiles exceptionally well. So what was his brand extension? A collection of fine wines.

Critics noted that it's not exactly common to see people sipping a Chardonnay or Merlot at NASCAR races. Branding experts pointed out that the extension diverged too far from his core brand.

This goes back to understanding how people perceive you, and what makes you unique (not only what you think makes you unique, but how others define your point of differentiation).

More Things to Consider

Just because you are an expert in one area does not mean that your personal brand will translate into another. Here are more points to ponder before extending a brand:

◆ Seriously assess your abilities. There are many cases of actors who, once they get famous, try to extend their brand into the music world. They record an album, and it's awful. They have diluted their brand.

◆ Think about the competition in the area you want to extend your brand. If that category already has a dominant presence, why take the risk?

◆ Consider whether the cost associated with a brand extension (research, marketing, product development) is worth the possible benefit.

◆ Make sure you have the financial resources available to fund the extension without draining the accounts of the core brand.

◆ Be absolutely certain that you can bring the same quality, expertise, trustworthiness, and consistency to the brand extension that you have with your core brand.

Brand Measurement

Before launching a brand extension, remember that you need to make sure your core brand is in good shape. That means taking into account how well you are doing. In other words, you need to measure your success.

How do you measure your success? Let us count the ways:

◆ Go back to your branding story. What's important to you? What are you trying to achieve?

◆ Review your plan every year to assess whether you are on target in achieving your goals.

◆ What is your attitude toward your brand? Have you been lazy in keeping your brand consistent and constant? Have you weakened the brand by cutting corners or merely counting on people to continue to do business with you instead of courting them?

Real World Brands

Over the past few years, *Brandweek* online readers have voted on the best and worst brand extensions of the year.

In 2007, the overall winner was PetSmart, which sells pet products. It started PetsHotel, a day-care and overnight facility for people's pets.

For the home category, La-Z-Boy won for its outdoor furniture brand extension.

For food, Curves, the women's-only fitness and health club franchise, won for its introduction of Curves Cereal.

The most inappropriate brand extension went to Precious Moments, which sells figurines and other collectibles, for offering, believe it or not, coffins. And voters named Hooters' energy drink as the worst food brand extension.

Another important way to measure if your plan is working is to evaluate your goals. Did you get the raise or promotion you were seeking in the allotted time frame? You can also seek feedback. Ask trusted friends and colleagues for input, for instance.

If you are satisfied that your brand is in solid shape, then it's time to think about a brand extension.

What If Your Brand Gets Huge?

What if everything goes as planned, and your brand becomes a far bigger success than you planned? Many people will say that is a good problem to have. Yet businesses through the years have failed because the demand for their products and services outgrew their ability to provide efficient customer care. Sometimes it's simply the inability to produce products as fast as customers want them that leads to a company's downfall.

What good marketing experts and corporate executives have learned is that internal structures must be in place for a brand to grow. The products must be available, transportation must be in place to get products to their destinations, and personnel must be working to oversee that the entire order and distribution process is effective.

If your brand is growing faster than you can handle, step back and rethink your process. The time may have come to get help. If you're an entrepreneur, it's not unusual to work 12- or 14-hour days, 7 days a week to get a business off the ground. But if you're putting in this many hours and it's not enough to keep up with demand, it may be time to build a team of dependable people who can help you out. Many entrepreneurs outsource work to independent contractors until their businesses are strong enough to hire a staff.

The Least You Need to Know

- Brand extension means launching new products or services based on your core brand.

- You can extend your personal brand by adding new services.

- Make sure the brand extension doesn't dilute your core brand.

- Measure the success of your core brand before starting a brand extension.

Chapter 16

Lessons from Megabrand Personalities

In This Chapter

- Mastering the basic skills of your profession
- Remaining relevant by shifting with trends
- Staying calm under pressure
- Taking risks

Celebrities such as Tiger Woods and Martha Stewart have become famous by building big personal brands. But getting to the top wasn't easy. Many celebrities have overcome huge obstacles to get where they are today. They were fired from jobs, told they would never succeed, or lost millions of dollars in a business deal gone bad.

In this chapter, we examine how certain superstars have built solid brands and the keys that keep them on top. Our examples range from politicians John McCain and Barack Obama to celebrities such as Katie Couric and Rachael Ray. Even if the last thing you want to achieve is fame, you can learn from these people's experiences to help strengthen your own personal brand.

Master the Basic Skills

The best way to build a super brand is simply to be better than any-body else at what you do. The first step in establishing that expertise is to understand what basic skills to hone until you are unequaled in your area of expertise. Nothing replaces mastering the basics of your field.

Although this advice may sound obvious, think about how many people skip over the basics.

Tiger Woods

As the story goes, Tiger Woods had a golf club in his hands soon after his birth on December 30, 1975. Under the disciplined tutelage of his father, the late Earl Woods, a lieutenant colonel in the U.S. Army, the boy developed extraordinary skills in hitting a golf ball. In fact, at age 2, he was a guest on the *Mike Douglas Show*, where he putted with legend-ary comedian Bob Hope. A year later, he scored 48 for 9 holes—a mark weekend golfers would be happy to achieve.

His national star began to ascend as an amateur, winning three U.S. Amateur titles and a team championship with Stanford University in 1994. Then, when he turned pro in 1996, he began to establish him-self as the most dominant athlete in perhaps any sport. Through 2008, Woods had finished first in 87 tournaments, including 65 on the PGA Tour. He had won 14 majors, trailing only Jack Nicklaus's 18. He has made more money—more than $81 million—in his career than anyone who has played the game, even though he is still in his early 30s!

While Woods has tremendous talent and drive—and an incredible abil-ity to perform well under pressure—he also constantly works on his game, putting in long hours refining his swing and putting stroke.

Real World Brands

Tiger Woods's stunning success as a golfer is but one element of his brand. He is good-looking and personable, and he's been scandal-free. His name is golden for his sponsors, which include Nike, American Express, and Accenture. His performance and classy demeanor have remained consistent since he first emerged on the national stage. He is one of the most recognized figures in the world.

Rachael Ray

While never claiming to be a chef, Rachael Ray first mastered the art of being a good, basic cook. She started her celebrity climb by teaching cooking classes at a gourmet food market in upstate New York. That led to a cooking gig on a local television station and a cookbook about 30-minute meals with a small publisher that sold well. Her big break came when she made an appearance on NBC's *Today Show*, which spun off into her own program on the Food Network called *30 Minute Meals*.

She extended her brand into magazines and kitchen products, as well as travel-related TV shows. She even extended her brand to music. She has also founded a nonprofit that encourages children to eat healthy meals.

Stay Relevant

History is littered with the names of flashes in the pan—people who rose to fame, only to be forgotten faster than the two guys who sang "Macarena." Yet there are certain people who figure out how to keep their personal brand relevant despite the changes in public taste and pop culture. Their brands are either strong enough to weather shifts in society or they are skilled at adapting to remain current. Here are three examples:

Madonna

A pop star, actress, author, and tabloid heroine, Madonna has built a brand based on constant change. Like a chameleon, she has adjusted her public persona to fit the times. She created her original brand as a naughty pop singer. Then she embraced the role of provocateur, publishing a book about sex called, well, *Sex*, featuring nude photos of her.

As she got older, she shifted her brand to embrace the fact that she had matured—becoming a mother (writing a series of children's books) and taking up spiritual pursuits through Kabbalah, the mystical offshoot of Judaism.

But not to let people think she had mellowed, she caused a sensation by kissing pop star Britney Spears on the 2003 MTV Video Music Awards. And then in 2008, when she was turning 50 and her career was perhaps waning, she thrust herself back into the headlines by having what was described as an "affair of the heart" with baseball superstar Alex Rodriquez, about 20 years her junior, which led to both of their divorces. (This happened just before she went on her latest tour.)

Madonna has consistently changed with the times, calculating her career moves to stay relevant in the pop world so that she can continue to sell her music and merchandise.

Real World Brands

Martha Stewart was a bored, stay-at-home mom in Westport, Connecticut, when she launched her catering business. Passionate about food since she was a child helping in the family garden, Stewart loved to cook and entertain with her husband.

In the early 1980s, after catering an affair with a faeries theme, an executive at Crown Publishing asked if she would write a book about food and parties. Since the release of *Entertaining* in 1982, Martha Stewart's name has become synonymous with homemaking. Her brand has expanded to television shows, magazines, and products for the home.

John McCain

In the summer of 2007, John McCain's bid to become the presidential nominee of the Republican Party looked hopeless. His campaign was in disarray and practically broke. The political pundits had written off the U.S. senator from Arizona, who just months earlier had been considered a frontrunner.

Yet McCain didn't give up on his pursuit to run as his party's candidate in the November 2008 election. He retooled his campaign by going back to what had made him a national presence during his presidential bid in 2000, when he became a media favorite for his Straight Talk Express, the bus on which he and reporters traveled. (Instead of isolating himself from the press, he engaged the journalists and answered all their questions. While Republican voters nominated George W. Bush instead in 2000, McCain established a national brand as a straight-shooter.)

For the 2008 primary, McCain focused his campaign on New Hampshire, holding, according to some estimates, 101 town hall meetings to meet with voters and answer their questions. He also went against popular opinion by backing President Bush's plan to increase troop levels in Iraq when people were clamoring to bring more soldiers home. McCain said he would prefer losing an election instead of a war.

By staying in the game, and staying true to his brand as a tenacious maverick, the American military hero, who spent five years as a prisoner during the Vietnam War, won the New Hampshire primary and eventually the Republican Party's nomination as its presidential candidate.

Big Risks May Pay Off

Steady and deliberate effort is the best way to build a personal brand. Sometimes, though, you might need to take quick action—seizing an opportunity to make your mark or even making bold moves from the start. In either case, you are taking big risks. Here are two examples that paid off huge.

President Barack Obama

The self-professed skinny guy with the funny name burst onto the national political scene with an inspiring, dynamic speech at the 2004 Democratic national convention. Barack Obama, a congressional member from Illinois, captivated a nation with the story of his rise from a broken household and grappling with racial identity (his mother was white, his father was from Africa). He was a star in the making.

But the 2008 Democratic slot for president had been reserved for Hillary Clinton, wife of two-term President Bill Clinton and a respected U.S. senator from New York. Clinton was destined for the White House, or so it seemed.

Obama, who turned 47 in 2008, was told to wait his turn—that he needed more experience. But he sensed that his message—change and hope—couldn't wait. So he chose to challenge the formidable Clinton machine for the Democratic nomination. And in a long and hotly contested race, he first stunned the favorite and won the party's primary to face election for the presidency. In another stunning instance, he won the presidency.

Obama sensed that his brand matched the tenor of the times and he moved forward when conventional wisdom counseled him to sit on the sidelines.

Donald Trump

A master of self-promotion, developer Donald Trump is perhaps the best-known businessman of his era. He learned early the importance of establishing a personal brand that is built on the premise that whatever he does is the biggest and the best.

Most of his properties—office buildings, golf courses, casinos, residences, hotels—bear his name. It's a big risk—and takes a big ego—to slap your name on every element of your life. There is no mistaking who is to blame when things go wrong. And things have gone wrong for Trump during his business career, including bankruptcy filings for some of his casinos in 2004.

But a lot has gone right, as exemplified by his vast real estate holdings in Manhattan, his bestselling business books, and his popular TV show, *The Apprentice*. No matter what you think of him, he has certainly established name recognition.

Have a Passion for Success

A common thread among many talented and well-known celebrity brands is that they have stayed focused through difficult times, never letting anything get in the way of their passion. Ralph Lauren was raised by hardworking parents in the Bronx and stayed focused on his passion for fashion. Ellen DeGeneres chose a life of comedy, and never let defeat keep her down for long. Both overcame many obstacles to achieve their personal success.

Ralph Lauren

Fashion designer Ralph Lauren is synonymous with quality, taste, and style. His clothing embodies the image of an Ivy League education, a Nantucket mansion, and a getaway in the Hamptons—the WASP ideal.

Yet Lauren grew up as Ralph Lifshitz, the son of Jewish immigrants who moved to the Bronx. His dad was a house painter. After serving in the U.S. Army, the young designer got his start as a clothing salesman and then opened his own tie store, where he developed a clothing line now famously known as Polo.

He had a vision for fashion design and a way of life that he passionately pursued. He expanded the brand to include home furnishings and even house paint. He now has a global presence and is one of the richest and most influential people in the fashion world.

Real World Brands

As odd as it may seem, personal brands as business ventures can continue long after a person has died. Take the late Elvis Presley, for instance. More than 600,000 people tour the beloved singer's home, Graceland, in Memphis, Tennessee, each year (only the White House gets more visitors to a private residence). And the King's music is still popular—more than 118 million record albums have been sold, behind only Garth Brooks and the Beatles. Not bad for a guy who died in 1977.

Ellen DeGeneres

New Orleans native Ellen DeGeneres quit college after less than a semester and decided to focus on a career in comedy. But success was elusive. There was a lot of hard work, nights spent in seedy comedy clubs around the country, and in 1997 a disappointing end to her first major television success, a sit-com called *Ellen*. DeGeneres and the character she played, named Ellen Morgan, simultaneously came out and announced that they were gay. The half-hour show failed the following year and DeGeneres thought her career was over.

But DeGeneres went back to work. She did more stand-up comedy and made special appearances. She thought she'd never again have a television show. That all changed in 2003 when DeGeneres was asked to launch *The Ellen DeGeneres Show*, a daytime talk show. By 2008, she had beaten Oprah Winfrey in the Harris Polls and had received several daytime Emmys, including Best Talk Show Host. DeGeneres is a good example of someone who worked hard and focused on her passion.

The Least You Need to Know

◆ Master the basics of your profession.

◆ Be prepared to take a big risk to elevate your personal brand.

◆ Stay focused and calm when it feels like you're failing.

◆ Be passionate about what you do.

Chapter 17

Global Responsibility

In This Chapter

- Understanding how globalization affects your brand
- Building a global brand
- Protecting your brand
- Respecting cultural differences

The world is shrinking, with companies outsourcing jobs and offshoring entire divisions, as well as individuals using cell phones and computers to communicate in real time across the globe. In addition, the changing economic and political systems of such emerging markets as China, India, and Eastern Europe have affected politics, business, and culture.

If there was any uncertainty about how interwoven the world economy is, the global financial crisis that started in the fall of 2008 removed those doubts.

Globalization can be seen as a threat (the loss of your job) or as an opportunity (a chance to expand your brand). In this chapter, we explore the importance of thinking globally while being mindful of cultural differences.

What Is Branding in a Global World?

In today's global economy, your brand is competing not only with someone in your city, but also with your counterparts in Asia, India, and elsewhere. More and more companies are outsourcing jobs—everything from customer service to basic accounting tasks—because they can be done cheaper overseas. If you work for a company that is shipping jobs offshore, it's vital you build a personal brand that has value for your employer.

That means you have to continue to update your skills by embracing lifelong learning and the willingness to make changes. And you have to remind your bosses and clients through words and actions that you bring value to the company with your talent and creativity—two things not easily outsourced.

Tips

The book largely credited with explaining the impacts of globalization is Thomas Friedman's *The World Is Flat*, which was published in 2005 and soon topped the *New York Times* Best Seller List.

These global changes also bring opportunities to expand your brand beyond your backyard. You can begin to beef up your reputation as a global citizen by increasing your awareness of international affairs.

Suppose you are employed at a college that conducts international business and develops global relationships. Even though you may not work in those areas, you can take steps to earn a reputation as someone with global interests. And when the time is right, you can make an aggressive push to get involved in the university's international endeavors.

So how do you start to think like a global citizen?

- Learn a second language. You can take classes or buy instructional tapes.

- Get a different perspective on current events by reading the foreign press, such as *The Economist* or the online version of *Japan Times* (in English), or listen to radio broadcasts by the BBC.

- Attend seminars or talks about international issues in your community.

◆ Volunteer at international festivals in your city.

◆ Act as a host family for high school or college students from foreign countries. (As a host family for college students from South Korea and Turkey, we have learned about different cultures and also met their friends from Vietnam and Bangladesh.)

◆ Take college classes (sometimes you can audit them for free) with international themes.

◆ Travel overseas.

◆ If your company has an international reach, volunteer to help out in those divisions.

If you build a reputation as a global citizen, you will begin to develop a network of international ties. And that networking may end up leading you to overseas opportunities—or at least working with overseas clients. For example, we have a friend who worked for a major manufacturing firm based in central Ohio. One of his duties was to oversee an engineering group in Mexico. He continued to live in Ohio and traveled on occasion to the Mexico plant to meet with his employees.

Following are a few other suggestions for beefing up your reputation as a global citizen.

Live Abroad

Sherry's sister and her family have made a habit of leaving their home in Colorado to live overseas for up to a year in such countries as Russia, China, and Spain. Through careful financial planning and tapping into their professional networks (he is a dentist; she is a health-care administrator), they have managed to put their jobs on hold in the United States and get employment in foreign countries. When their only child was school age during one of their journeys, she attended an English-speaking school.

The family has developed ongoing relationships with people around the world, and their travels have benefited Sherry's sister and her husband professionally and personally.

Study Overseas

To remain competitive for good jobs, more and more college students are seeking international experience. One way to get this experience is to study abroad; many colleges have programs that will allow students to attend classes at foreign universities or at their own campuses in other countries.

High school students also can participate in exchange programs that permit them to live with a family and attend school in a different country (Rotary International sponsors a popular exchange program).

International Internships

Another way to gain international exposure is through internships with overseas companies. College students can get those on their own, or work with a company such as University of Dreams, which sets up the internship, housing, and more for a (hefty) fee.

Before our daughter's senior year of college, she spent two months in Barcelona interning with a marketing company. In doing so, she enhanced her resumé, learned about a new culture, and improved her Spanish skills.

Without that experience, she felt she couldn't compete as strongly with other candidates when she graduated from college.

What Makes a Global Hit?

There are people with huge global personal brands, such as Bill Gates and Nelson Mandela. And then there are the rest of us.

But even if you aren't a software genius or a beacon of political courage, you can still take steps to expand your brand globally.

You can use technological advances such as e-mail, websites, and blogging to reach across borders. For instance, you can send electronic newsletters to a client in Bangalore, India, just as easily as to your next-door neighbor—all for the same cost.

One of the wonders of this global reach is that nobody knows how big or small you are—just whether you can get the job done. A one-woman shop can act big by contracting work out through national or international collaborations: your designer could be in California, your writer in Canada, and your proofreader in Illinois.

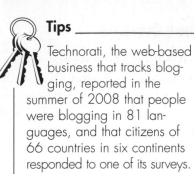 **Tips**

Technorati, the web-based business that tracks blogging, reported in the summer of 2008 that people were blogging in 81 languages, and that citizens of 66 countries in six continents responded to one of its surveys.

And global opportunities are increasing for small shops. In fact, according to a study by the U.S. Small Business Administration, exports by American small businesses have increased from $100 billion to $400 billion between 1992 and 2008.

For example, a small store in our hometown specializes in climbing gear and sells its products to customers around the world through the Internet. Here's another one: After graduating from college in California in 1999, Jacquelyn Tran started an online business for the small perfume store run by her parents. Sales at Beauty Encounter increased from $150,000 to $20 million in 2007, with 15 percent coming from the United Kingdom, Canada, France, Germany, Latin America, and Japan.

And there's the case of Sherry's sister, whom we mentioned earlier. She launched her global brand by volunteering for a committee that hosted foreign health-care professionals. Through those relationships, she received invitations to speak in Australia and travel to China and Spain. In Spain, she worked on a project that became the inspiration for a similar study—funded by a large grant—in her home state of Colorado. Then she co-wrote a paper about the study that was published in a prestigious European medical journal.

Strong branding can elevate your standing in the global marketplace. And your brand will be enhanced if you are skilled at doing business abroad.

The Next Level

If you are a small business owner and are considering selling your service or product in another country, you face an uphill battle. After all, going global means you are asking people to buy something from someone they don't know—and to stop buying from someone they are familiar with.

Real World Brands

We came across a story about a Dutch consultant who posed a simple question on the Internet and ended up starting a business relationship with a Chinese manufacturer. It is a good example of how you can grow a global brand without leaving your house.

The consultant, using LinkedIn, sent a message asking fellow LinkedIn users for advice on how to improve the performance of his battery in his iPhone. A Chinese manufacturer responded by touting its battery, which the consultant bought. The consultant posted a note about the product on LinkedIn, and he began to get queries from other users asking where they could buy the battery. The consultant contacted the manufacturer and made arrangements to be its U.S. distributor for the battery.

So from a simple posting, he started a battery sales company. He also sent a message to the president of LinkedIn about the collaboration, and the company's publicist spread the word. *The New York Times* published a story about him.

Think about some of the same questions large corporations ponder before they launch an international presence:

- Does your product or service address a global need?
- Can your product or service fit the characteristics of that country (taste, ritual, income)?
- How big is the market in that country?
- What is the growth potential?
- How profitable will this venture be?
- Could expensive shipping be an issue?
- How politically stable is the market?
- Are there people you can partner with in that country?

Brand Protection

In this era of easy access to information from around the world, it is vital to protect your ideas (and, thus, your brand). We aren't lawyers, so we won't pretend to give legal advice. But consider the following when thinking about giving your brand legal protection.

Register your trademark. A *trademark* or *service mark* is essentially a brand name, and you need to protect it from being copied.

def•i•ni•tion

According to the United States Patent and Trademark Office (USPTO), a **trademark** includes any word, name, symbol (like a logo), or device used, or planned to be used, for commercial purposes to identify and distinguish your goods from goods manufactured or sold by others—and to indicate the source of the goods. A trademark is called a **service mark** if it deals with a service instead of goods.

One of the benefits of registering your trademark is that, according to the USPTO, you possibly can use it to obtain registration in foreign countries. See the USPTO website for a thorough explanation of that process.

To learn everything you ever wanted to know about federal trademarks, visit uspto.gov/web/offices/tac/tmfaq.htm. You also can find a free download of *Basic Facts About Trademarks* at uspto.gov/web/offices/tac/doc/basic. If you are interested in patents, go to uspto.gov/main/patents.htm. The appropriate agency for copyrights is the United States Copyright Office in the Library of Congress. For information on that process, visit copyright.gov.

Avoiding the Language Barrier

A huge obstacle to developing a global brand, and one of the more frustrating elements of working in an international arena, is language. Unless you are fluent, you will definitely feel out of your element from time to time.

> ### Real World Brands
>
> In the United States, a marketing campaign by Kraft Foods for Oreos was based on nostalgia: it involved a commercial of a parent teaching a child the traditional way of eating the cookie by twisting it apart, licking off the creamy center, and dunking it in a glass of milk.
>
> Kraft had to adjust its marketing campaign for Oreos in China, however, because parents had no history with the snack. The ads focused on the *children* teaching the parents how to twist, lick, and dunk.

Big brands work hard to overcome language barriers. But sometimes even they don't get it right. According to one report, Pepsi tried to market its soft drink in Taiwan years ago with the slogan "Come Alive—You're in the Pepsi Generation." Unfortunately, the translation of the phrase had a different meaning. Pepsi was promising to bring people's ancestors back to life.

If you need to convert your writing into another language, don't use a dictionary to translate each word literally. You will end up looking foolish. There are nuances to each culture's language that a dictionary just can't convey. You might want to hire a professional translator who understands the language and the cultural adaptations to avoid accidentally embarrassing yourself or, worse, offending your audience.

Careful with Clichés

When speaking with someone who doesn't use English as a first language, American idioms probably won't make any sense. Imagine a person not familiar with English trying to figure out the meanings of "The early bird gets the worm" or "all thumbs" or "barking up the wrong tree."

> ### Real World Brands
>
> Interbrand, a brand consulting corporation, rated the world's most valuable brands for 2008. The top five were Coca-Cola, IBM, Microsoft, GE, and Nokia.

David C. Thomas, a professor at Simon Fraser University in British Columbia, Canada, studies cultural intelligence, which essentially is how people deal with other cultures. How knowledgeable and mindful are you of cultural differences, and do you have the skills to react appropriately?

It is a matter of recognition, accommodation, and assimilation, among other things. Some of the questions he poses to gauge a person's cultural intelligence include …

- ◆ Do you understand people's feelings?
- ◆ Can you deal with delays calmly?
- ◆ Do you stay relaxed when trying to talk to someone from another culture?
- ◆ Are you empathetic to the difficulties someone from a different culture may be experiencing in a new country?

Mixed Messages or Worse

Although the world may be getting smaller, marketing studies show that we are not living in a homogeneous world. Local tastes and cultures still matter. In fact, some experts say that people are embracing traditional customs more as a backlash to globalization.

So it's not just language you need to be aware of. Your body language and other actions can send unintended messages. Here are a few examples of Western traditions taking on different meanings in other countries:

- ◆ In Thailand, the head is a sacred place. Touching the top of it is considered insulting.
- ◆ Making the OK symbol is some countries is not okay. In France, it means worthless.
- ◆ Showing the sole of your shoe to an Arab is an insult.
- ◆ In Poland, Germany, and Sweden, carnations are for funerals.
- ◆ In the Far East, the order of a person's family name comes first instead of last.
- ◆ Giving a clock as a gift in China might be considered the same as wishing for bad luck for the recipient.
- ◆ It is appropriate for men in the Mediterranean, North Africa, and the Middle East to kiss each other on both cheeks.

◆ Pointing, as well as direct eye contact, is considered rude in several Asian countries.

It is a good idea to study the cultures and customs of the region before conducting business. You don't want your brand to be tarnished by your actions.

The Least You Need to Know

◆ While globalization can be viewed as a threat, it also can be an opportunity for building your brand.

◆ Your personal brand can go global thanks to technology and international collaborations.

◆ Register your trademark.

◆ Be mindful and knowledgeable about cultural differences.

Chapter 18

The Smoke and Fog of Branding

In This Chapter

- ◆ Understanding the importance of brand authenticity
- ◆ Overcoming skepticism
- ◆ Creating a portfolio of personal anecdotes
- ◆ How hyper-competition affects your brand

It seems like it would be easy to create the illusion of a personal brand in today's hyper-connected world. An illusion of a brand is an inauthentic brand. It's a brand in which components have been fabricated, such as awards that have been made up, jobs that were never held, or activities that never occurred.

Websites, blogs, 24-hour news channels, e-mails, text messaging, and other social networking tools have made it seem easy to build a personal brand. Yet society for a variety of reasons has become more skeptical about information it receives. People are more likely now than ever before to check out the credentials of someone they meet. They are more likely to look up facts online, even if they have just read them in a newspaper, to confirm their reliability. They question data in advertisements. The same tools that boost your brand can also be used to check up on it. Thus, you should be prepared to prove that you are a capable person who can accomplish the tasks or deliver the products that you promise.

To ensure authenticity during a job search, for example, be sure that the information on your resumé matches the information online. If you choose to eliminate information from your resumé that may be revealed with an Internet search, be prepared to answer questions about it. For instance, we know a woman with a Ph.D. in psychology who has chosen to leave this information off her resumé because she is afraid prospective employers will think she is overqualified. Maybe that's the case, but if someone in human resources discovers the omission, she'll have to explain her reasoning.

In this chapter, we talk about the importance of maintaining the authenticity of your personal brand. Although it's sometimes tempting to fabricate facts and statistics associated with your personal brand, doing so can bring harsh results.

Setting the Stage

The Internet has opened the door wide for people to take on alternative personas. Not only has the Internet given rise to online games involving avatars living in virtual worlds, it has also made it easier to create false personas. In other words, the tools are available to enable anyone to create a fake brand should they choose to do so.

Just being aware of your brand, whether you have worked hard to create it or it has just naturally evolved, will help you begin to take control over it.

Increasing Skepticism

In 2006, bloggers discovered that Wal-Mart was paying two people to write gushing reports in a fake blog about the chain's stores. The discovery was a public relations disaster for the behemoth retailer because it exposed the company as being inauthentic: instead of actual customers writing good comments online, the company had to pay people to do it.

Since then, the act of *flogging*—fake blogging—has become taboo for online marketers.

Real World Brands

Someone we're sure never knew he had a brand was a former auto mechanic in our hometown. He was the type of guy who hardly smiled and spoke sparingly. Not exactly Mr. Sunshine. But he had a good business. Why? He was honest, reasonably priced, and competent. You knew you'd get a fair deal and, in almost all cases, he'd fix the problem with your vehicle. Customers knew there would be no surprises when they dealt with him. Without even realizing it, this grumpy auto mechanic had built a brand. His customers quickly got over his personality. When he retired and shut down his shop, his longtime customers were the ones feeling grumpy.

Now don't get us wrong: we're not encouraging you to turn your smile upside down when dealing with colleagues or clients. Our point is that the mechanic had formed a strong bond with his customers because he offered consistently good service at a reasonable rate.

And during the 2008 presidential campaign, people could—and did—check the truthfulness of claims made by and about the presidential candidates by visiting www.factcheck.org, a website established by the University of Pennsylvania's Annenberg Public Policy Center.

This need for authenticity on the part of consumers may be part of a natural evolution of this country's most dynamic generation, the Baby Boomers. A Philadelphia think tank called the Center for Cultural Studies and Analysis says that every 20 years people question themselves and begin redefining their personal identities. It is a gradual process as a person attempts to establish his or herself at a particular age and place in time. As the Baby Boomers enter their 50s and 60s, they have started a search for personal identity. They have entered an era of personal reevaluation.

Gen X and Gen Y have joined the search for authenticity perhaps due to other factors. We are in an era during which banks have failed, toys from China have been found to contain lead, and our pet food has been contaminated. Today's younger generations are demanding to know where their products are coming from and what they are made of.

Major corporations are frantically searching for ways to convince consumers that their brands are authentic. Across generations, Americans are searching. They want the truth. And they want to be able to trust in the companies they do business with.

Uphold Your Reputation

In the early chapters of this book, we mentioned that your personal brand is much like your reputation. Most people work hard at making contacts and proving that they are capable of holding responsible jobs.

Personal, one-on-one networking can still be your most valuable form of communicating your personal brand. For instance, we once met a communications specialist who made a great first impression as a nice guy. He was so pleasant and helpful, in fact, we thought it might have been an act: surely, he's just trying to win us over and, after he's gotten what he wants, we'll never hear from him again. But his behavior has remained consistent through the years. And colleagues echo each other in praising him as the nicest guy you'll ever work with. Besides being good at his job, his consistent, one-on-one behavior has helped him build a personal brand as a considerate, thoughtful, and authentic professional.

We also are acquainted with a powerful attorney who doesn't hesitate to promote himself or his projects when talking with people. At first, some folks might discount his accomplishments because he isn't afraid to talk about them. But his achievements are noteworthy. You won't hear him bragging about the small stuff or inflating his victories. He knows that doing so would raise questions about the authenticity of his brand. People know that what he's touting is worth paying attention to.

Don't Be Seduced by the Internet

Don't let the anonymity of the Internet seduce you into exaggerating your skills or padding your resumé.

If you're trying to get your foot in the door of a profession, be honest about your skill level and experiences. Get to know people you admire and those you would like to work with. Let them see your skills first-hand. Being open and honest may land you an entry-level job that can lead to true professional success.

The Story of Jayson Blair

While he was attending the University of Maryland in the 1990s, a journalism student named Jayson Blair built a big personal brand. He was a chatty, affable young fellow and showed a lot of talent for reporting. He interned with *The New York Times* and continued to correspond with that newspaper when he returned to college.

When the *Times* offered Blair a full-time job, he quit college just shy of graduating, moved to New York City, and went to work for the paper. He had accomplished what very few other young journalists had the opportunity to do: he got a full-time job as a reporter at one of the country's top newspapers. Because of that, he became a legend at his former college.

Months later, Blair's *Times* editors assigned him to cover the Beltway sharpshooters who were killing people in the Washington, D.C., area. At the time, nobody knew who the shooters were.

Blair, it seemed, was getting tips that none of the other local media could get. He was beating reporters from the *Washington Post* and other Washington-area news media in their own region. This made his competitors suspicious. They—and others—began a quiet investigation into his reporting tactics.

Editors at the *Times* were suspicious, too, and began their own investigation. They discovered hundreds of erroneous articles written by Blair. Eventually, the 27-year-old shamefully resigned his position, admitting that he had lied.

Editors at the newspaper were deeply embarrassed. Not only had Blair ruined his own personal brand, he had damaged the newspaper's brand, too. The executive editor and managing editor both resigned soon after. Sadly, Blair's ordeal led to his eventual mental and emotional breakdown.

The lesson? Back up your personal brand. Never present yourself as something you are not, and never give your competition a reason to suspect that your personal brand is anything less than 100 percent authentic.

Creating Your Own Anecdote

One way to increase the authenticity of your brand is to create a portfolio of anecdotes. That is, have some stories you can tell in casual conversation with colleagues that fortify your professional reputation.

We know a high school teacher who likes to talk about his adventures in the classroom. One of our favorites is about an incident early in his career. He wanted to do something that would grab the students' attention and let them know he wasn't a typical teacher. So without comment, he stood on a table in his classroom and began to lecture. It was all the students could talk about afterward. When he tells that anecdote, he's letting people know he's an unconventional teacher.

We also know a woman who travels extensively for her work with the military. She tells a story about being in Poland for a conference several years ago. One night she was awakened by a strange sound in her room. She didn't discover its source at first, but later learned that someone—most likely a spy—had been in her room snooping around. The anecdote adds a bit of intrigue to her personal brand.

Of course, if you embellish your anecdotes and get caught, your brand's authenticity will be questioned.

Today's Hyper-Competition

Today's workplace is hyper-competitive. There is heightened competition to get a job and keep it. Competition to get the next promotion. Competition to get the next contract.

If you work hard and stay authentic to your personal brand, you will have a good chance at being successful. But don't expect success overnight. The economy is sluggish, the jobless rate is higher than it has been in the last two decades, and companies are closing their doors. You must prove that you have the skills and acumen to be a top performer.

Enter Web 2.0. We are now living in the open-source world where we should expect to receive comments and criticism via the web. When we get it, it should not surprise us. Millions of bloggers are now talking about brands that they like and brands that they dislike. They may be talking about you, the product you offer, or the service you provide. The beauty and the beast of Web 2.0 is that input is allowed—and even encouraged.

Warning

If you attempt to create a false persona, or even to present a brand that has no substance to it, your competition will notice, and they will be more than happy to expose your weaknesses, your failings, and your inauthenticity. Be sure that your professional experiences are deep enough, your personal affiliations strong enough, and your emotional bonds with your target audience tough enough to withstand the scrutiny.

The Least You Need to Know

◆ The web makes it easy to create an illusion of a brand.

◆ There is increasing skepticism in today's society.

◆ Today's workplace is hyper-competitive.

◆ Don't be a fake or give your competitors a reason to suspect you are a fake.

Chapter 19

Being Your Own Brand Barista

In This Chapter

- Becoming a brand manager
- Keeping your online presence fresh
- Fixing your online reputation
- Managing your tone
- Maintaining brand discipline during plateaus

You've put a lot of work into establishing and developing your personal brand. You have written your branding story and learned how to communicate over the clutter.

But your work is not finished. Just like routine maintenance and regular check-ups are essential to keeping your house and car looking good and running smoothly, maintaining your brand is essential.

You will need to continue to tweak, perhaps even overhaul, your brand to keep up with the times. Managing your brand is just as important as putting your plan in place. This chapter offers tips for keeping your brand sharp and current.

What Is a Brand Manager?

Companies that care about brands staff a position called a brand manager. A brand manager is responsible for maintaining a company's brand. He or she makes sure the brand is on point and all facets of a business are working toward the same branding goal.

As a one-person brand, you are your own brand manager. And although you don't have other divisions to help you manage your brand, at least the meetings will be a lot shorter.

What Is Your Online Brand Image?

The easiest way to check your online brand image is to plug your name into a search engine and review the results. This is important because prospective employers, new clients, and even new acquaintances will do the same. (Check out both Google and Yahoo! You might be surprised at the difference in the listings.)

What pops up on the first page? Are they the items that best describe your brand?

Tips

Go to careerdistinction.com/onlineID to learn to analyze the results of your Google search. It presents five descriptions of your web presence to help you figure out if you need to revamp your online brand message.

How to Fix Your Online Brand Image

We know of a college graduate who almost didn't get a job because of content found on a search engine. A column he had written for his college newspaper was posted without his knowledge on a blogger's site. The blogger added a couple of paragraphs to the top of the opinion piece, including some highly offensive language about women.

Unfortunately, these statements read as if they were part of the original column.

The prospective employer could have dismissed him as a candidate based solely on that posting. But he contacted the candidate, who explained the situation and proved he wasn't responsible for the offensive language.

So if something similar happens to you, how can you fix the problem?

♦ Contact the site directly and ask its operators to remove the posting.

♦ Hire an online reputation management company that will inundate the web with positive information about you to push the negative items lower on the list of search results. Some studies show that most people stop looking at search engine postings after the first three pages.

♦ Don't post embarrassing photos or write offensive blogs to begin with.

♦ If there's nasty stuff on a blog about you, join the conversation by pointing out what is wrong, but don't come off defensive about every negative comment. Choose your battles.

> **Warning**
>
> A 2007 study by ExecuNet showed that 83 percent of recruiters in the United States checked out job candidates online. And 43 percent of them said they eliminated candidates if they found unfavorable information about them.

> **Tips**
>
> Plug your name into a program such as Google Alerts, which will send you an e-mail when your name appears on the web—whether it's in a media release, on a company website, or within a blog. Such features help you manage your personal brand.

Protecting Your Facebook Info

If you use Facebook or MySpace to share photos and stories with close friends that you don't want anyone else to see, at least try to do the following:

♦ Be choosy about whom you select as a friend. You can even create two lists, one for the chosen few and the other for everyone else.

♦ Establish an alias that only your closest friends know.

Keeping It Fresh

In an interview published in *Advertising Age*, newly hired ConAgra senior vice president of advertising Dave Linne talked a lot about how the company's products—Pam cooking spray, Reddi-wip, Egg Beaters, Chef Boyardee, Hunt's, Orville Redenbacher—were household names, but not viewed as current. In fact, he called them underachievers. His said his job was to develop a new advertising campaign to revitalize those lines.

You must analyze your brand in the same way. Ask yourself: Am I too reliant on past success? Sure, I've won the awards, gotten the big promotion, received the raise and recognition, but what recent accomplishments can I point to with pride?

You should periodically review your personal branding plan to make sure it is staying current with trends in your industry. Here are a few things to think about:

♦ Do your business cards look outdated?

♦ Do you attend seminars and conventions about your industry?

♦ Do you read the latest trade journals?

♦ Do you post fresh content on your blogs? (Spend at least about 30 minutes a week adding new entries.)

♦ Is your LinkedIn profile current?

♦ Do you review your file of performance reviews, correspondence from clients or colleagues, etc.?

The Mic Is Never Off

Keep in mind that your personal brand is always "on." No matter what you are doing or where you are, you are making an impression. Anything you say or do can have an impact.

To borrow a line from the broadcasting industry: the mic is always on. In other words, you should never say anything that you wouldn't want your audience to hear.

A recent example of how damaging it is to ignore this advice came during the summer of the 2008 presidential campaign. Remember the controversy that broke out over the Rev. Jesse Jackson's comments about Barack Obama? He was appearing with another guest on a Fox News program and during a break Jackson thought he was no longer "on." But he was. His comment to the guest was: "Obama talks down to blacks. I want to cut his nuts off."

His remarks made national headlines, of course, and they tarnished his personal brand. Albeit controversial and not without previous stumbles, Jackson is a revered civil rights leader and two-time presidential candidate. But this vulgar statement gave ammunition to pundits and others to blast him and speculate on his motivations. The conclusions were harsh, ranging from jealousy to arrogance; many people said that he was more concerned about hanging on to his own status than helping the new wave of minority leaders make it to the top.

Whatever the motivation, Jackson's misstep diminished his personal brand.

Be Careful with E-mail

Most of us have done it: written a snippy, snarky comment for a friend about someone else's e-mail … but mistakenly hit "reply" instead of "forward," sending the message to the person you were making fun of. Oops. No matter how much you apologize, the receiver won't ever forget or perhaps forgive.

Warning

Generally speaking, if you work for a public body, such as a county or state office, your e-mails are part of the public record, which means anyone who asks for copies can read them. So what you write in an e-mail at work could end up being reprinted in the newspaper.

In 2008, the attorney general of Ohio, Marc Dann, learned this lesson the hard way. Highly embarrassing work e-mails he exchanged with a female employee were published in newspapers across the state. Dann later resigned for issues related to how he ran his office.

Brand Management and Your Boss

For people who work for someone else, your career path primarily depends on your boss, whether he or she is a genius or an idiot. Your boss determines whether you get promoted, whether you get a raise, whether you get the challenging high-profile assignments. Your boss also talks to other bosses. His or her one-sentence statement about you will be your brand with other division heads who might control your future when you want a job in another part of the company.

Your success at work is heavily influenced by your boss's interpretation of your brand. While nobody wants to be a suck-up, nobody wants to be viewed as a slacker, either. Bosses want people who make their jobs easier: getting jobs completed competently and on time and giving them good advice.

It also helps if your boss views you as trustworthy and loyal. It might mean the difference between getting a promotion or being bypassed—and keeping your job during tough times. But you also don't want to be a pushover. Pick your battles when you disagree. No boss likes a complainer, so choose to go to the mat on only those issues that are most important to you.

You also may have to play some politics, even if you find it unseemly. It doesn't hurt to try to make your boss look good (unless, of course, he or she is unethical, a liar, or dishonest—then all bets are off). Never embarrass your boss even if you are right, and never criticize him or her to a co-worker. Those comments most likely will spread and perhaps make their way back to your boss—and be a lot more severe than what you actually said.

Managing Your Tone

Your words are one thing. The way you say them is another. People will believe tone over message. Sarcasm, cynicism, and anger have their place. But it must be the right place, the right time.

Speaking loudly comes across as being annoying and bossy. Speaking softly makes you appear weak. Slow talkers may look less than bright. Fast talkers may come across as trying to sell something nobody wants. Find a middle range.

Tips

Aristotle once said, "It is easy to fly into a passion—anybody can do that. But to be angry with the right person to the right extent and at the right time and with the right object and in the right way—that is not easy."

Working While Not at Work

The owner of a high-powered public relations firm we know was invited to attend a major sporting event in 2008 with some close friends. She was all set to enjoy the activity. Then she learned another guest was one of her clients. She was disappointed because she felt as if she were back on the clock.

The point is that even during nonwork settings you may often find yourself in the company of clients or co-workers. Your behavior at the company softball game or the going-away party for Fred in accounting will be judged by others. If you drink too much at the going-away party, you might become the story at the office the next day. If you take the softball game too seriously or pout if you don't do well, people might question your leadership skills. Same goes for dinner parties with acquaintances in the community.

Managing Your Brand During Dry Spells

A lot of the time you spend building your career may feel wasted. Those climatic, dramatic breakthrough moments happen irregularly. Mostly, you are traveling on level ground, your star not rising consistently.

During these flat periods, you need to be patient and maintain confidence in your brand plan. It's essential to keep managing your brand during those plateaus, even if it doesn't feel like much progress is being made. Without the discipline to manage and maintain your consistency, your brand will begin to unravel, and you may not be in a position to take advantage of a big opportunity.

Don't Get Stuck

You must constantly work to keep your brand from getting stale. One way for it to begin to wither is to stay in a job with no prospects for advancement. Perhaps you like the work and your colleagues. But you've been passed over a few times for promotions, or the raises just aren't coming as frequently as you'd like. That sends a signal that while you may be valued (it's easier for your boss to keep you on the job than to train someone else), you aren't seen as capable of bringing more value to the company.

 Warning

Building a brand as the top leader in a family-owned business can be difficult if you are not related to the ownership. In the end, the family usually wins. The best interests of the family almost always override the best interest of the employee.

Your brand also might be in danger if you earn a big paycheck in a middle management role. Over time, your boss may begin to think someone younger (and cheaper) could do the same job just as well.

In either case, it may be time to start looking for a new career challenge.

Building a Reservoir

A key part of maintaining your brand is building a reservoir of goodwill. You do so by establishing an impressive record of accomplishments. You also are trustworthy and consistent. You make sure the people who influence your career are aware of your record so that when something bad happens (and something bad will) your brand won't be diminished entirely.

It's like the college basketball coach who has had a couple of losing seasons. He is more likely to keep his job if has run a clean program, had previous winning seasons, and is well received by the press and fans. If he has a reputation for being surly and cutting corners, when trouble comes, that reservoir of goodwill may be dry.

Keep your reservoir full by consistently maintaining your brand.

Handling Failure and Coming Clean

It's tough enough to polish and sustain a brand when things are going good. But things aren't always going to go smoothly. How you deal with failure is a great test of your brand. In some cases, it could even enhance your reputation.

Take Lolo Jones, for example. The U.S. Olympic athlete looked as if she were going to win the 100-meter hurdles during the 2008 summer games in Beijing, China. Then she hit the next-to-last hurdle with her foot, throwing her off-stride. That little mistake pushed Jones back in the pack. She went from a gold medal to seventh place just like that. Imagine training for four years and coming so close, but failing in the end.

Not much later, she appeared on NBC's *Today* program with her American teammate, Dawn Harper, who won the race. Sitting next to Harper, who was wearing a gold medal like a necklace, Jones showed remarkable poise and composure as she described her heartache. She talked about when she cried at home while watching the 2004 Olympics because she hadn't made the team—and noted the irony of crying again after the 2008 race. Then she said she hoped that in four more years she would cry one more time at the Olympics, only these would be tears of joy after winning a gold.

At the end of the interview, it was Jones who viewers would remember for her grace under pressure.

As we've said before, authenticity is vital to building a strong personal brand. Sometimes we screw up. Admit it. Come clean. Consumers have seen too many examples of big companies who try to hide their mistakes and then lose a lot of brand equity (and millions of dollars in sales and lawsuits) when their misdeeds are exposed. If you are going to be trustworthy, you have to own up to your mistakes.

Revitalizing Your Brand

Styles and tastes change. We take things for granted or get a little lazy. Time lapses and one day you realize your brand is a bit frayed, like a favorite pair of jeans you've worn too long.

Or your company may have been sold and suddenly you have new owners to impress. Perhaps the skill sets that found you favor with the previous boss aren't necessarily as appreciated by the new one. You may have to adjust your brand plan to meet the expectations of your new boss.

The best way to revitalize your brand is to return to the basics. Go back to the same procedures you executed when you began to build your brand.

- ◆ Who are you? (Determine whether your skills and the services you offer have changed.)
- ◆ Go back to the people you originally talked to about your brand and see if their perceptions about you are different.
- ◆ What is your niche? What makes you unique?
- ◆ Have you remained consistent in your branding?

You may end up just tweaking your brand to keep it up-to-date. But you might also need to overhaul your plan. It sounds daunting, but it may be necessary if your original plan no longer is working.

T. Boone Pickens built a fortune as an oilman and corporate raider. In 2004, he funded the so-called Swift Boat ads that attacked Democratic presidential nominee John Kerry's military career in Vietnam. Environmentalists and Democrats considered him less than an ally. In fact, the top Democrat in the U.S. Senate, Harry Reid of Nevada, called Pickens his "mortal enemy."

Four years later, in 2008, Pickens had revamped his brand—at the age of 80, no less. The man who earned billions in the oil business was pushing for a radical reworking of the country's energy policy. He believed that the United States should decrease its dependence on imported oil and invest instead in domestic energy sources, especially wind. He was planning to build the world's largest wind farm in the Texas panhandle.

To gain support for his ideas, he recruited environmentalists and Democrats, including Senator Reid. He also launched a massive publicity blitz to explain his change of mind. So now the oil wildcatter has rebranded himself as a green advocate.

The Least You Need to Know

- Maintaining your brand is about control and consistency.

- Update your blogs regularly.

- Routinely check out your listings on search engines.

- Remember that your boss plays a big role in how your brand is perceived.

- It may be necessary to tweak or overhaul your brand if it has become outdated.

Chapter 20

Branding in the Future

In This Chapter

- ◆ Maintaining brand flexibility
- ◆ Identifying the fastest-growing jobs
- ◆ Valuing creativity
- ◆ Sustaining your brand

As we've noted throughout the book, drastic changes taking place throughout the world are making it vital for people to figure out and communicate their value to their clients, colleagues, and supervisors.

In this chapter, we explore ways to prepare for change over the next few years. We discuss the importance of creativity, flexibility, and sustainability in a world that will continue to be reshaped by technological advances. And we touch upon the way social responsibility could impact your personal brand.

Remaining Flexible in a Changing Economy

A major part of life is dealing with transitions. How well you adapt to those transitions will determine how successful you are.

The future of your personal brand depends on your ability to be flexible. You will need to stay on top of sociological, economic, and scientific trends.

You have to continue to innovate and generate positive emotional appeal. Your brand is your best asset in a future driven, perhaps, by continued outsourcing and economic uncertainty. And it helps to be flexible in this ever-evolving world.

Adjusting Your Personal Brand in an Economic Crisis

Shifts in society sometimes occur that fundamentally alter people's lives. Just imagine if you were in the financial services sectors during the fall of 2008 when the global economic crisis first took hold. Massive instability forced unprecedented moves by the U.S. government to arrange for mergers and engineer bailouts. Seemingly overnight venerable institutions went bankrupt (Lehman Brothers) or were sold (Merrill Lynch). Even before the meltdown, more than 200,000 jobs had been cut by financial companies since the start of 2007. According to news stories, college seniors at the end of 2008 with majors in business and finance were looking to go to law school or even find jobs overseas until the economy improved.

Then there's the newspaper industry. Because of the rise of the Internet and the fall of the economy, daily newspapers have been battered the past few years as readership and ad revenues declined. Thousands of journalists lost jobs in 2008. Two of the largest newspaper chains in the United States announced massive layoffs. Gannett cut more than 1,700 positions and McClatchy eliminated almost 2,500 jobs.

Obviously, that's not good news for reporters and editors. But journalists have highly desirable skills in a knowledge economy: they can gather information and write about it concisely, clearly, and accurately. Now, it's a matter for those unemployed journalists to apply those skills in different fields, such as public relations or doing research for private investigators.

Others have started their own communications businesses. And some writers have discovered that blogging is a natural fit for them (although it may take time to be profitable). Before, they were constrained by space and the inclinations of an editor or a publisher. As bloggers, they are their own editors and publishers. Good reporters writing about important and interesting topics will find a following. And they can do so on their time and as their own boss.

Growing Categories for Brands

As you manage your brand for the future, you should be aware of the hot career fields. One good place to find out is the U.S. Department of Labor. Its Bureau of Labor Statistics issued a report projecting the job market until 2016.

Total employment is expected to increase 10 percent, from about 150 million jobs in 2006 to 166.2 million in 2016. As expected, the American economy will continue to move from producing goods to providing services. The fields projected to experience the most growth will be, in order:

◆ **Education and health services:** Combined, these two fields are expected to grow by 18.8 percent, adding nearly 5.5 million jobs. Of those jobs, 4 million will be related to health care and social assistance, driven by the aging of the Baby Boomers. In fact, the report states that more than 3 out of 10 new jobs created in the United States will be in this sector.

> **Tips**
>
> The U.S. Department of Labor forecasts that 7 of the 20 fastest-growing occupations by 2016 will be related to health care.

◆ **Professional and business services:** This category is projected to grow by 23.3 percent and add 4.1 million new jobs. The largest industry growth in this sector will be employment services, at 692,000 new jobs. The Labor Department attributes the growth, in part, to the need for highly specialized human resources services.

Also expected to experience significant job growth is the field of computer systems design and management, as well as scientific and technical consulting services.

◆ **Information:** This category includes software publishing, Internet publishing and broadcasting, plus wireless telecommunication carriers, motion picture production, and newspaper/periodical/book/directory publishing.

◆ **Leisure and hospitality.** Nearly 80 percent of the new jobs in this sector will be in the fields of amusement, gambling, and recreation.

Other fast-growing categories include government, financial activities, and trade/transportation/utilities.

Here is a list of the top 15 fastest-growing occupations from 2006 to 2016:

◆ Network systems and data

◆ Communications analysts

◆ Personal and home care aides

◆ Home health aides

◆ Computer software engineers (applications)

◆ Veterinary technologists and technicians

◆ Personal finance advisers

◆ Makeup artists, theatrical and performance

◆ Medical assistants

◆ Veterinarians

◆ Substance abuse and behavioral disorder counselors

◆ Skin-care specialists

◆ Financial analysts

◆ Social and human service assistants

◆ Gaming surveillance officers and gaming investigators

◆ Physical therapist assistants

Ingenuity Valued: The Creative Class

One of the prized assets in today's knowledge-based economy is creativity. And we're not talking about how well you can paint a picture or perform on the stage. We mean your ability to solve problems, recognize trends, and generate new ideas. Your level of creativity is a distinguishing factor in how bright your star shines.

Richard Florida, the author of the bestselling and highly influential book *Rise of the Creative Class*, argues that the key to cities prospering in the future is attracting and retaining creative people. He also claims that the city in which you choose to live will have a profound impact on your life.

He believes that the more creative a city's population, the better chance it has of prospering. He reasons that creative people are vibrant, open-minded, innovative, and willing to take risks. Those qualities are attractive to highly educated people. And that kind of environment will lead to economic vitality and social harmony.

Tips

Ingenuity is vital to solving problems. Distinguished Canadian academic Thomas Homer-Dixon wrote a book called the *Ingenuity Gap* that raised the question of whether there are enough good ideas to meet the challenges of an increasingly complex and fast-paced world.

It is a theory that has taken hold with city officials and urban planners across the country. And there is a push in metro areas to make cities more attractive to this creative class.

How does this affect your personal brand? The sharper your creative skills, the more in demand you will be. And following Richard Florida's theory, your choice in where you live should be determined not by just your job, but also by whether the psychology of a city is best suited to your brand. For instance, if you are a political scientist, then consider moving to Washington, D.C., since it is home to 78 percent of the political scientists in the country.

Creativity in Action

The following are three examples of creative ideas. Two resulted in highly unlikely businesses, and one (about water, of all things) attacked a serious global problem.

Life Is Indeed Good

Bert and John Jacobs founded a company in Needham, Massachusetts, in 1994 based on a sense of optimism. Doesn't exactly sound like your typical business plan.

Reminiscent of the smiley face of the 1970s, they created a grinning cartoon stick figure named Jake. They paired Jake with the motto "Life is Good" on some T-shirts. The buoyant attitude in the face of complex times caught on. In 2007, they sold 4.2 million shirts for $25 apiece. They now also sell coffee mugs, hats, beach towels, dog bowls, backpacks, and more. Sales were expected to hit $135 million in 2008.

Their business is built on more than products, though. It's a philosophy of life. There are now Life is Good festivals across the country, with one in Boston attracting about 30,000 people in 2008. The festivals also raise money for children's charities (about $3 million so far).

Play Goes Big

Charlie Todd formed Improv Everywhere in New York City in 2001 to bring joy and chaos to public places. His idea centered on injecting a sense of playfulness into a life driven too much by work and duty.

One of his stunts involved sending 207 people into Grand Central Terminal with the instructions to freeze in place at the exact same time for five minutes—and then unfreeze and act as if nothing had happened. In another case, people periodically got on a subway car, with no pants on. Another time, participants drifted into a bar throughout one night and treated an unsuspecting customer as if it were his birthday.

The other interesting part of Improv Everywhere is that the events depend on whoever shows up after reading about them on the group's website.

Todd's idea has caught on with at least one company looking for creative ways to market itself. In September 2008, Improv Everywhere signed a sponsorship deal with Yahoo!.

Tap Water for $1

New York ad man David Droga came up with a simple response to a massive problem: the billion or so people in the world without clean water, which is the second leading killer of children younger than 5.

Partnering with UNICEF, he started the Tap Project. Various restaurants in New York City agreed to ask patrons to do one thing: add $1 to their bill if they drank a glass of tap water they normally would get for free.

The idea caught on with other cities, and there are now plans to go international. In its first year (2007), the program raised more than $5 million for UNICEF.

Among the various honors he has received for the Tap Project, Droga won *Creativity* magazine's top award in 2008.

Your Long-Term Brand Sustainability

When hard times hit, strong brands survive and weak brands fail. What are the keys in the future to sustaining your personal brand? We turn to some advice from author and communications consultant Tim Kitchin.

In the book *Beyond Brands*, to which he contributed one of the essays, he writes that there are five core principles of brand sustainability for corporations. They are organizational agility, market sensitivity, value fit, brand relevance, and stakeholder collaboration.

Tips

The Iroquois tribe believes that, "In our every deliberation, we must consider the impact of our decisions on the next seven generations." Talk about brand sustainability.

That same framework can be applied to personal brands.

- ◆ **Organizational agility:** Are you able to change your own habits and your way of thinking? Can you make changes to meet new circumstances?

- ◆ **Market sensitivity:** Are you able to recognize market changes?

- ◆ **Value fit:** Are you prepared—if your target audience has diminished or disappeared—to find new clients?

- ◆ **Brand relevance:** How significant is your presence in your community?

- ◆ **Stakeholder collaboration:** Do you have the ability to create and communicate a vision that others in your community can follow?

If you can answer "yes" to these questions, then the odds of creating a sustainable brand—one that lives up to its promises—will increase.

Underlying Branding Themes

There's more to developing a personal brand than building a career or increasing revenue in your own business. What are the other themes of your brand? Consider the late Paul Newman. He was admired for his great acting abilities. But he also was revered because he expanded his brand to helping people. His Newman's Own food products have raised $250 million to fund thousands of charities. His underlying brand theme was social responsibility.

And social responsibility is becoming a growing concern in this age of ecological (melting ice caps, weird weather) and economic (growing disparities between the rich and poor) uncertainties.

Tips

Even corporations understand that social responsibility can enhance their brands. A recent survey released by the Natural Marketing Institute in Pennsylvania reported that 60 percent of the 2,000 adults surveyed said they felt more loyalty to companies that are socially responsible. And 38 percent said they would pay more for products produced by those businesses.

Personal Brand Evolution

We can't emphasize enough the dramatic and revolutionary impact of the Internet on how we will live in the future. The deep and forceful changes in the communications industry will affect many related fields as well.

Here's one small example regarding television viewing. In the fall of 2008, *Saturday Night Life* featured skits with Tina Fey impersonating Republican vice-presidential candidate Sarah Palin. In the past, almost everyone would have watched the show on TV at 11:30 on a Saturday night. Hence, if you were an advertiser interested in appealing to that particular audience, you knew how to reach them.

But that's not the case anymore. Slightly more than half of the people who watched one of the skits didn't see it on TV. They saw it somewhere on the Internet: YouTube, NBC.com, or Hulu.com. If you are an advertiser, what's the best way to reach that audience now?

Here's another example: according to a marketing study, mothers between the ages of 32 and 43 rely on traditional means of making decisions—word of mouth. Mothers ages 19 to 31, however, depend on blogging or e-chats.

These shifts in how people learn and communicate will affect your ability to build relationships, engage with people, and maintain your brand. The shift to Web 2.0 means people are going online to participate in shaping public opinion, with big brands having less control over their messages and images. Gen X and Gen Y, born between 1977 and 1996, have grown up with the Internet. They are the digital generation. They don't just sit there and absorb the culture, they engage it, create it, shape and critique it.

All of these factors will force you to evaluate your brand and consider how your skills and mind-set have to evolve. Change is difficult, but it also can be exciting. For your brand to thrive, you need to remain flexible while adhering to the basics of consistency and trustworthiness.

And remember that your brand is more than your service or product. It's also about forming branding relationships in a fragmented world so you can accomplish something bigger than yourself.

The Least You Need to Know

◆ Remain flexible in the face of change.

◆ Creativity will make you stand out.

◆ Social responsibility is an asset to your brand.

◆ The Internet will continue to change the way people think, act, and communicate.

Glossary

alignment   A design element that helps bring order to a printed page.

anecdote   An incident or event that is interesting or amusing.

blog   A website that features ongoing entries usually related to one topic.

blogger   Someone who writes a blog.

blogging   The act of writing a blog.

blogosphere   The virtual community of all blogs posted on the Internet.

brand authenticity   Staying true to and consistent with your branding statement.

brand equity   A phrase that describes the value your brand holds.

brand evangelists   Deeply committed customers and fans of a brand. They create excellent word of mouth about the brand and its extensions.

brand extension   The process of launching new products or services based on your core brand.

brand identity   The visual and verbal ways that a brand is identified.

brand imaging   The psychological associations attached to a brand.

brand immersion   This occurs when a target audience is given an experience that provides them with firsthand knowledge about your brand.

brand loyalty   The strong, positive feelings a customer has toward a product or person.

brand management   The process of making sure a brand is controlled and consistent.

brand manager   A person or group that oversees a brand to make sure it stays consistent with its brand message.

brand message   A clear, simple statement that explains your expertise.

brand perception   This is how people see your brand.

brand position   How a brand compares with the competition.

brand positioning manager   A person who is aware of other brands and knows that a brand is built around a unique product that fits into the whole corporate scope.

brand positioning statement   A brief sentence or two that describes your personal brand.

brand relevance   A phrase pertaining to the personal qualities that make a person attractive to a target audience.

branding   The process used to build a positive emotional response.

branding statement   A introduction to a branding story, focusing on a brand's strengths.

buzz marketing   A term describing the word-of-mouth endorsement of a product.

call to action   A request that the target audience respond.

communication channels   Various ways that people communicate, including phone, text, print, broadcast, websites, blogs, etc.

cultural intelligence   A term describing how knowledgeable a person is regarding cultural differences.

domain   The unique name of an Internet address, such as www.penguin.com.

e-mail blast   This is a way to send a group e-mail.

effective messaging   The verbal and visual cues selected to represent a brand accurately.

electronic newsletters   A formatted newsletter that can be sent via e-mail.

elevator pitch   A short statement about a brand, generally used by those in sales.

emotional resonance   The emotional connection a brand has with its target audience.

Facebook   A social networking site.

Flickr   A photo-sharing website.

flog   A fake blog set up by a company to promote a product or brand.

flogging   The act of fake blogging.

focus group   A group discussion about a specific product, service, or cause.

frame   The way a message is communicated.

functional advantage   What makes a brand stand out among others.

Google   A popular Internet search engine.

guerrilla marketing   An unconventional way of spreading the word about a product or service.

halo effect   A term describing a positive perception of a company.

hierarchy of needs   A theory that says humans have a variety of needs, from basic to very complex ones.

LinkedIn   A social networking site used mainly by professionals.

marketing   A way to persuade people to purchase a product or service, or join a cause.

marketing survey   A way to test the public's response to a new product before considering its release.

media advisory   Announcement of an upcoming event that the media may want to cover.

media relations   Techniques that are used by public relations professionals to communicate a brand through the media.

media release   An announcement sent to the media.

media strategy   An action plan regarding how you will advertise your brand.

MySpace   One of the most popular social networking sites.

name recognition   When your name is linked with your face and your abilities.

news hole   The amount of space left to fill after the ads have been placed in a publication.

online reputation management company   A business that will try to remove or push down negative listings on a search engine about a company or individual.

op-ed columns   The opinion pieces that run on the page opposite the page that carries the newspaper's editorials.

pdf   Portable document format created by Adobe systems frequently used to transport documents or artwork via the Internet.

personal brand   How you view yourself and how others view you.

podcast   A video or audio broadcast over the Internet that can range from the amateur to the very professional.

search engine optimization   The process of improving the volume of traffic on a website.

signature line   A name and other information that can be formatted to appear at the end of e-mails.

target audience   A group of people to whom a brand is focused.

trademark   A brand name, symbol, or device that is registered with the United States Patent and Trademark Office.

Twitter   A program used to send text messages to a group of people.

verbal identity   The way a person expresses him- or herself with language and writing skills.

Vimeo   A website similar to YouTube where videos can be posted.

viral marketing   The way products, services, and causes are easily forwarded to others on the web through e-mail blog postings, etc.

visual identity   The obvious part of a brand that you can see, including graphic components such as logo, fonts, colors, and typefaces.

vlog   A blog that is done in a video format, instead of being written.

Web 2.0   The current era of web use in which people can comment and critique through blogs, wikis, podcasts, websites, and social networking sites.

web conferencing   A meeting or training session that includes computer visuals.

webcast   Streaming video that appears online. It can be used as an advertising vehicle, but not always.

webinar   A web conference.

white space   The space on a designed page that includes no graphic or text.

wiki   A web page or collection of web pages designed to allow a group of people to contribute.

wild posting campaign   A way to spread the word about a product or service by using posters, decals, or other temporary means.

Yahoo!   An Internet search engine.

YouTube   A website where videos can be posted.

Appendix B

Resources

Books

Arruda, William, and Kirsten Dixson. *Career Distinction: Stand Out by Building Your Brand*. Hoboken, NJ: John Wiley & Sons, 2007.

Beals, Jeff. *Self Marketing Power*. Omaha: Keynote Publishing, 2008.

Breakenridge, Deirdre, *PR 2.0: New Media, New Tools, New Audiences*. Upper Saddle River, NJ: FT Press, 2008.

Clifton, Rita, and John Simmons, eds. *Brands and Branding*. Princeton, NJ: Bloomberg Press, 2004.

D'Alessandro, David F.. *Brand Warfare: 10 Rules for Building the Killer Brand*. New York: McGraw-Hill, 2001.

———. *Career Warfare: 10 Rules for Building a Successful Personal Brand and Fighting to Keep It*, New York: McGraw Hill, 2008.

Friedman, Thomas L. *The World Is Flat: A Brief History of the Twenty-First Century*. New York: Farrar, Straus and Giroux, 2005.

Gilmore, James H., and B. Joseph Pine II. *Authenticity: What Consumers Really Want*. Boston: Harvard Business School Press, 2007.

Ind, Nicholas, ed. *Beyond Branding: How the New Values of Transparency and Integrity Are Changing the World of Brands*. Sterling, VA: Kogan Page, 2004.

Ireland, Susan. *The Complete Idiot's Guide to the Perfect Resumé, Fourth Edition*. Indianapolis: Alpha Books, 2006.

Levinson, Jay Conrad. *Guerrilla Marketing: Easy and Inexpensive Strategies for Making Big Profits from Your Small Business, Fourth Edition*. Boston: Houghton Mifflin, 2007.

Peters, Thomas J. *The Brand You 50, or, Fifty Ways to Transform Yourself from an "Employee" into a Brand That Shouts Distinction, Commitment, and Passion!*, New York: Knopf, 1999.

Ries, Al, and Laura Ries. *The Origin of Brands: Discover the Natural Laws of Product Innovation and Business Survival*. New York: HarperBusiness, 2004.

Shiffman, Denise. *The Age of Engage: Reinventing Marketing for Today's Connected, Collaborative, and Hyperinteractive Culture*. Ladera Ranch, CA: Hunt Street Press, 2008.

Tybout, Alice M., and Tim Calkins, eds. *Kellogg on Branding: The Marketing Faculty of the Kellogg School of Management*. Hoboken, NJ: John Wiley & Sons, 2005.

White, Sarah E. *The Complete Idiot's Guide to Marketing, Second Edition*. Indianapolis: Alpha Books, 2003.

Williams, Robin. *The Non-Designer's Design Book*. Berkeley, CA: Peachpit Press, 1994.

Websites

Adage.com

The website for *Advertising Age*, which covers the advertising and media industries.

BLS.gov

Web home for the Bureau of Labor Statistics in the U.S. Department of Labor.

Brandchannel.com

Run by Interbrand, a brand management company, it advertises itself as "providing a global perspective on brands."

Brandweek.com

The website for the weekly publication that covers the branding industry.

Careerdistinction.com

The website for the authors of *Career Distinction*, William Arruda and Kirsten Dixson.

Gmarketing.com

Home of the site run by Jay Conrad Levinson, known as the father of guerrilla marketing.

Marketingprofs.com

Marketing professors and professionals share insights.

Myownbrand.com.hk

A website based in Hong Kong for Asian professionals, but it has an interesting quiz called "How Strong is Your Personal Brand."

Shiftingcareers.blogs.nytimes.com

A *New York Times*–sponsored blog about shifting careers.

Summerinternships.com

Website for the University of Dreams summer internship program.

Technorati.com

The go-to site for blogging information.

Wired.com

Website for *Wired* magazine.

Associations

American Marketing Association
www.ama.org

National Retail Federation
www.nrf.org

Rotary International
www.rotary.org

Small Business Administration
www.sba.gov

Toastmasters International
www.toastmasters.org

Index

A

Abercrombie & Fitch, 24
accomplishments on resumés, 59
accuracy of resumés, 60
achievements, 103
ad representatives, 147
advertising
   ad representatives, 147
   advantages, 146
   channels, 148
      airplane banners, 154
      billboards, 154
      broadcast, 148-149
      bumper stickers, 153
      buttons, 153
      direct mail, 152
      endorsements/sponsorships,
         153
      newspapers/magazines, 151
      personal letters, 153
      posters, 154
      T-shirts, 154
      telephone books, 152
      webcasts, 149
      websites, 150-151
   demographics, 148
   examples, 146-147
   media strategies, 146
   personal needs, 147
   planning, 155
airplane banners, 154
alignment in design, 45
Allison, Julia, 165
alternative newspapers, 102

Amnesty International guerrilla
   marketing example, 165
anecdotes, 204
appearances, 86-87
Aqua Teen Hunger Force guerrilla
   marketing example, 166
Arbitron, 148
Armstrong, Heather B., 130
association building
   communities, 80
      churches, 81
      involvement, 77
      neighborhoods, 83
      parent-teacher organizations,
         82
      political, 81
      volunteering, 83
      youth sports, 82
   joining boards, 80
   lunch appointments, 79
   media, 80
   perceptions and power, 76
   professional associations, 79
   professional conferences, 79
   public speaking, 80
   social networking, 77-78
   workplace, 79
audiences, target
   connections, 35
   earning trust, 35
   entertaining
      event sponsorships, 94
      hosting, 92-94
      minglers, 92
   needs, 28-29

reaching
  depth of knowledge, 30-31
  emotional bonds, 31-32
  functional advantages, 29-30
relating to, 33
researching, 160
talking to, 40-41
authenticity, 12-13
  Blair, Jayson example, 203-204
  creating anecdotes, 204
  false personas, 200
  honesty, 202
  hyper-competition, 204
  increasing skepticism, 200-202
  realism, 13
  Starbucks, 12
  true self, 13
  upholding reputations, 202
  Wal-Mart blogging incident, 200

B

Baby Boomers, 134
balance, 23
Basic Facts About Trademarks
  download, 195
Beauty Encounter, 193
Ben & Jerry's identity, 51
best/worst brand extensions, 179
biking guerrilla marketing
  example, 164
billboards, 73, 154
Blair, Jayson, 203-204
blogger, 122
blogging, 122
blogs, 130, 140-142
  advertisements, 150-151
  posts, 122
body language, 90
  eye contact, 90
  handshakes, 90
  international cultures, 197-198
  stance, 91

book writing, 106
Boston treasure hunt guerrilla
  marketing example, 167
brand equity, 8
brand evangelists, 177
brand extension, 172
  best/worst examples, 179
  cautions, 178
  celebrity chefs, 173-174
  consistency, 177
  cult brands, 177
  examples
    Buffett, Jimmy, 173
    Clorox, 172
    Ivory soap, 172
    Kovel, Ralph and Terry, 173
  growth, 179
  measuring core brand success,
    178
  starting points, 175-176
brand loyalty, 8
brand management, 6, 208
  dry spells, 213
  e-mail cautions, 211
  family-owned businesses, 214
  handling failure, 215
  jobs with no prospects for
    advancement, 214
  managers, 18
  mic is always on, 210
  nonworking settings, 213
  online brand images
    checking, 208
    fixing, 208-209
    protecting on social net-
      working sites, 209
  reservoirs of goodwill, 214
  revitalization, 215-216
  someone else, 212
  staying current with industry
    trends, 210
  tone, 212

brand positioning, 5, 25
Brandweek online, 179
Branson, Richard, 175
broadcast advertising, 148-149
broadcast media, 103
brochures, 70
Buffett, Jimmy, 173
building
    anecdotes, 204
    associations
        communities, 77, 80-83
        joining boards, 80
        lunch appointments, 79
        media, 80
        old-school social net-
            working, 77-78
        perceptions and power, 76
        professional associations, 79
        professional conferences, 79
        public speaking, 80
        workplace, 79
    brands, 14
    public relations plans, 118-119
    reservoirs of goodwill, 214
    trust, 35
bulk mail, 152
bulletin boards, 72
bumper stickers, 153
business cards, 66-68
business publications, 102
buttons, 153
buzz marketing, 159

C

Career Distinction online identity
    calculator website, 208
Carilao, Maria, 163
cases for portfolios, 62
celebrities
    brands, 7-8
    chefs, 173-174

megabrand examples
    DeGeneres, Ellen, 187
    Lauren, Ralph, 187
    Madonna, 183
    McCain, John, 184-185
    Obama, Barack, 185
    Ray, Rachael, 183
    Stewart, Martha, 184
    Trump, Donald, 186
    Woods, Tiger, 182
cell phone calls, 138
Chicago Cubs, 6
Chicago video game guerrilla
    marketing example, 166
Child, Julia, 174
choosing
    personal brands, 5
    portfolio cases, 62
church associations, 81
clean water creativity example, 225
Clemens, Roger, 7
clichés, 196-197
Clorox example, 172
clothing, 86-87
coaching youth sports, 82
columnists, 106
communication
    body language, 90-91
    creativity, 42
    good design
        alignment, 45
        contrast, 45
        proximity, 44
        repetition, 45
        white space, 45
    marketing collateral
        billboards, 73
        brochures, 70
        bulletin boards, 72
        business cards, 66-68
        letterhead, 69
        marketing kits, 71-72

postcards, 70
signature lines, 68-69
new methods
blogosphere, 140-142
cell phone calls, 138
e-mail, 134-136
generations, 134
instant messaging, 137
Skype, 143
social networking sites, 140
text messaging, 138-139
web conferencing, 143-144
wiki, 142
one-on-one, 47
simple messages, 41
talking to the audience, 40-41
verbal identity, 46-47
visual identity, 43
web evolution, 227
community associations, 80
churches, 81
neighborhoods, 83
parent-teacher organizations,
82
political, 81
volunteering, 83
youth sports, 82
conferencing via the web, 143-144
connecting with target audiences,
35
consistency in brand extension,
177
Consumer Reports, 8
contrast in design, 45
core brand success, 178
corporate retail resumé example,
54
cover letters, 61
creating. *See* building
creativity, 42
future, 223-225
guerrilla marketing, 161

cult brands, 177
cultural differences, 196-198
current with industry trends, 210

D

daily newspapers, 101
Deen, Paula, 174
DeGeneres, Ellen, 187
demographics for advertising, 148
demystifying the media, 100
broadcast, 103
print, 101-102
depth of knowledge, 30-31
Derrie-Air guerrilla marketing
example, 164
design, 44
alignment, 45
contrast, 45
personal websites, 123
portfolios, 62
proximity, 44
repetition, 45
white space, 45
Dictionary of Marks, 173
differentiation
depth of knowledge, 30-31
functional advantages, 29-30
diffusion theory in public relations, 111
dinner manners, 88-89
direct mail advertisements, 152
domain names, 124
Droga, David, 225
dry spells, 213

E

e-mail, 134-136
blasts, 126
caution, 211
etiquette, 136

education and health services
fields, 221
electronic newsletters, 125
elevator pitches, 22
emotional bonds with target audiences, 31-32
emotional resonance, 31
endorsements, 153
entertaining
hosting events, 92-94
mingling, 92
sponsorships, 94
equity, 8
etiquette, 87
dining, 88-89
e-mail, 136
follow-ups, 89
texting, 139
thank you's, 89
evangelists, 177
evolution of the Internet, 227
evolving market needs, 33
expertise
fields, 9
establishing, 176
messaging, 34
messaging, 34
extending brands, 172
best/worst examples, 179
cautions, 178
celebrity chefs, 173-174
consistency, 177
cult brands, 177
examples
Buffett, Jimmy, 173
Clorox, 172
Ivory soap, 172
Kovel, Ralph and Terry, 173
growth, 179
measuring core brand success,
178
starting points, 175-176

extreme marketing. *See* guerrilla
marketing
eye contact, 90

F

Facebook, 23, 127-128
FactCheck.org website, 201
failure, 215
false personas, 200
family-owned businesses, 214
fast-growing fields, 221-222
federal trademarks website, 195
feet-on-the-street marketing. *See*
guerrilla marketing
fields
depth of knowledge, 30-31
expertise, 9
establishing, 176
messaging, 34
fast-growing, 221-222
mastering basics
Ray, Rachael, 183
Woods, Tiger, 182
one-on-one communication, 47
figuring out personal brands, 5
fixing online brand images,
208-209
flexibility in changing economy,
220-221
flogging, 201
Florida, Richard, 223
follow-ups, 89
framing messages, 110
Friedman, Thomas, 190
functional advantages, 29-30
future
fast-growing fields, 221-222
flexibility in changing economy, 220-221
ingenuity, 223-225
sustainability, 225-226
web evolution, 227

G

Gen X/Y, 134
globalization
    brand protection, 195
    clichés, 196-197
    cultural differences, 196-198
    Friedman, Thomas, 190
    international internships, 192
    iPhone battery example, 194
    language barriers, 195-196
    living abroad, 191
    mixed cultural messages, 198
    Oreo campaign example, 196
    overview, 190
    preparations, 194
    starting, 190
    studying overseas, 192
    successful, 192-193
    Western traditions with differ-
        ent international meanings,
        197-198
goals on resumés, 57
good design, 44
    alignment, 45
    contrast, 45
    proximity, 44
    repetition, 45
    white space, 45
Gordon, Jeff, 177
grassroots marketing. *See* guerrilla
    marketing
growth preparations, 179
guerrilla marketing, 158
    creativity, 161
    defined, 158
    examples
        1960s, 163
        Allison, Julia, 165
        Amnesty International, 165
        biking, 164
        Derrie-Air, 164
        multimillion-dollar bra, 164
        pop-up businesses, 165
        T-shirt exposure, 164
        Yo-Yos, 163
    laws, 165
        Aqua Teen Hunger Force
            example, 166
        Boston treasure hunt, 167
        Chicago video game, 166
    partnerships, 162
    planning, 159
    repetition, 161
    researching target audiences,
        160
    subsets, 158
    word of mouth, 162

H

halo effect, 75
handling failure, 215
handshakes, 90
hierarchy of needs in public rela-
    tions, 111
Homer-Dixon, Thomas, 223
honesty, 202
hosting social events, 92-94
hosting TV/radio programs, 107
hot career fields, 221-222
hyper-competition, 204

I

identities
    Ben & Jerry's, 51
    portfolios, 62
    resumés, 52
        accomplishments, 59
        accuracy, 60
        compared to personal web-
            sites, 62

corporate retail example, 54
cover letters, 61
experiences, 58
goals, 57
organizing, 53-55
proofreading, 60
readability, 59
respiratory health-care
    worker example, 55
verbal, 46-47
visual, 43
IM (instant messaging), 137
immersion, 42
Improv Everywhere, 224
information fields, 222
ingenuity, 223-225
Ingenuity Gap, 223
instant messaging (IM), 137
Interbrand, 196
international
    exposure
        brand protection, 195
        clichés, 196-197
        cultural differences, 196-198
        Friedman, Thomas, 190
        international internships,
            192
        iPhone battery example, 194
        language barriers, 195-196
        living abroad, 191
        mixed cultural messages, 198
        Oreo campaign example, 196
        overview, 190
        preparations, 194
        starting, 190
        studying overseas, 192
        successful, 192-193
        Western traditions with dif-
            ferent international mean-
            ings, 197-198
    internships, 192
voice calling system, 143

Internet forums, 131
iPhone battery example, 194
Ivory soap example, 172

J-K

Jacobs, Bert and John, 224
Jarvis, Greg, 176
Jones, Lolo, 215

Kovel, Ralph and Terry, 173

L

Lagasse, Emeril, 174
language barriers, 195-196
Lauren, Ralph, 187
laws and guerrilla marketing, 165
    Aqua Teen Hunger Force
        example, 166
    Boston treasure hunt, 167
    Chicago video game, 166
leisure and hospitality fields, 222
letterhead, 69
letters for public relations, 115
Levinson, Jay Conrad, 158
"Life Is Good" motto, 224
Limited Brands, 10
LinkedIn, 128
living abroad, 191
loyalty, 8
lunch appointments, 79

M

Madonna, 183
magazines, 101, 151
managing brands, 6, 208
    dry spells, 213
    e-mail cautions, 211
    family-owned businesses, 214

handling failure, 215
jobs with no prospects for advancement, 214
managers, 18
mic is always on, 210
nonworking settings, 213
online brand images
    checking, 208
    fixing, 208-209
    protecting on social networking sites, 209
reservoirs of goodwill, 214
revitalization, 215-216
someone else, 212
staying current with industry trends, 210
tone, 212
manners, 87
dining, 88-89
e-mail, 136
follow-ups, 89
texting, 139
thank you's, 89
marketing collateral
billboards, 73
brochures, 70
bulletin boards, 72
business cards, 66-68
letterhead, 69
marketing kits, 71-72
postcards, 70
signature lines, 68-69
marketing kits, 71-72
mastering field basics, 182
    Ray, Rachael, 183
    Woods, Tiger, 182
McCain, John, 184-185
measuring core brand success, 178
media
advisories, 114-115
consultants, 107
exposure
    becoming a source, 104-105
    broadcast media, 103

examples, 100
hosting TV/radio programs, 107
media consultants, 107
print media, 101-102
publicizing achievements, 103
writing books, 106
writing columns, 106
kits, 117
releases, 112-114
strategies, 146
men's clothing, 80, 87
messaging
creativity, 42
evolving market needs, 33
expertise, 34
framing for public relations, 110
good design, 44
    alignment, 45
    contrast, 45
    proximity, 44
    repetition, 45
    white space, 45
instant messaging, 137
marketing collateral
    billboards, 73
    brochures, 70
    bulletin boards, 72
    business cards, 66-68
    letterhead, 69
    marketing kits, 71-72
    postcards, 70
    signature lines, 68-69
simple, 41
talking to the audience, 40-41
text messaging, 138-139
verbal identity, 46-47
mic is always on, 210
Millenial generation, 134
mingling at social events, 92
mommy blogs, 130

multimillion-dollar bra guerrilla marketing example, 164
MySpace, 127-128

N

needs for personal brands, 4
neighborhood associations, 83
networking
  events
    hosting, 92-94
    mingling, 92
    presence, 95
    sponsoring, 94
  old-school, 77-78
  online, 127
    blogs, 130
    Facebook, 127-128
    Internet forums, 131
    LinkedIn, 128
    MySpace, 127-128
    protecting online brand images, 209
    sites, 140
    Twitter, 129
    vlogs, 131
    YouTube, 129
new communication methods
  blogosphere, 130, 140-142
    advertisements, 150-151
    posts, 122
  cell phone calls, 138
  e-mail, 134-136
    blasts, 126
    caution, 211
    etiquette, 136
  generations, 134
  instant messaging, 137
  Skype, 143
  social networking sites, 140
  text messaging, 138-139
  web conferencing, 143-144
  wiki (Wikipedia), 142

Newman, Paul, 226
newspaper advertising, 151
Nielsen website, 148
nonworking social settings, 213

O

Obama, Barack, 127, 185
old-school social networking, 77-78
one-on-one communication, 47
online brand images
  checking, 208
  fixing, 208-209
  protecting on social networking sites, 209
opinion columns, 115
Oreo campaign example, 196
organization on resumés, 53-55

P

parent-teacher organizations, 82
ParentTalkToday.com blog, 141
passion for success, 187
patents, 176
people's marketing, 158
perception, 23-24
personal assessment, 9
personal branding statements, 18
personal branding stories
  summarizing into elevator pitches, 22
  writing
    examples, 20
    input from others, 20
    personal questions, 17
    reasons for, 14-15
    reflection, 19
    reputation, 16-17
    statements, 18
personal brands, 4
personal letters, 153

personal websites, 123
  compared to resumés, 62
  designing, 123
  domain names, 124
  search engine optimization, 124
  tracking visitors, 124
photos for publicity, 116-117
Pickens, T. Boone, 216
planning
  advertising, 155
  guerrilla marketing, 159
podcasts, 126-127
political community associations, 81
pop-up businesses guerrilla marketing example, 165
portfolios, 62
positioning, 24
  Abercrombie & Fitch, 24
  positioning statement, 25
postcards, 70
posters, 154
power, 76
presence at social events, 95
Presley, Elvis, 187
print media, 101-102
printed materials
  good design, 44
    alignment, 45
    contrast, 45
    proximity, 44
    repetition, 45
    white space, 45
  marketing collateral
    billboards, 73
    brochures, 70
    bulletin boards, 72
    business cards, 66-68
    letterhead, 69
    marketing kits, 71-72
    postcards, 70
    signature lines, 68-69
professional and business services, 221

professional associations, 79
professional conferences, 79
proofreading resumés, 60
protection, 195
proximity in design, 44
publicity photos, 116-117
publicizing achievements, 103
public relations, 110
  diffusion theory, 111
  framing messages, 110
  hierarchy of needs, 111
  media kits, 117
  plans, 118-119
  publicity photos, 116-117
  tools, 112
    letters/opinion columns, 115
    media advisories, 114-115
    media releases, 112-114
public speaking, 80

Q-R

quick conversation, 78

Ray, Rachael, 183
readability of resumés, 59
realistic self, 13
Redenbacher, Orville, 8
relating to target audiences, 33
relevancy, 183
  Madonna, 183
  McCain, John, 184-185
repetition
  design, 45
  guerrilla marketing, 161
reputation, 16-17
  Stewart, Martha, 16
  upholding, 202
researching target audiences, 160
reservoirs of goodwill, 214
respiratory health-care worker resumé example, 55

resumés, 52
  accomplishments, 59
  accuracy, 60
  compared to personal websites, 62
  corporate retail example, 54
  cover letters, 61
  experiences, 58
  goals, 57
  organizing, 53-55
  proofreading, 60
  readability, 59
  respiratory health-care worker example, 55
reviewing brands, 210
revitalization, 215-216
Rise of the Creative Class, 223
risk taking, 185
  Obama, Barack, 185
  Trump, Donald, 186

S

search engine optimization, 124
self-examination, 9
self-knowledge, 13
Sena, Kathy, 141
service marks, 195
signature lines, 68-69
simple messages, 41
skepticism, 200-202
Skype, 143
social networking
  events
    hosting, 92-94
    mingling, 92
    presence, 95
    sponsoring, 94
  old-school, 77-78
  online, 127
    blogs, 130
    Facebook, 127-128
    Internet forums, 131

    LinkedIn, 128
    MySpace, 127-128
    protecting online brand images, 209
    sites, 140
    Twitter, 129
    vlogs, 131
    YouTube, 129
source for media
  becoming, 104
  interview tips, 105
  relationships, 105
sponsorships, 94, 153
stance, 91
Starbucks, 12
starting
  brand extension, 175-176
  globalization, 190
staying relevant, 183
  Madonna, 183
  McCain, John, 184-185
Stewart, Martha, 16, 184
Stewart, Rollen, 163
stores as brand extension, 176
studying overseas, 192
success
  core brand, 178
  globalization, 192-193
  passion, 187
super brands
  mastering field basics, 182-183
    Ray, Rachael, 183
    Woods, Tiger, 182
  passion for success, 187
  staying relevant, 183
    Madonna, 183
    McCain, John, 184-185
  taking big risks, 185
    Obama, Barack, 185
    Trump, Donald, 186
sustainability, 225-226

T

taking big risks, 185
  Obama, Barack, 185
  Trump, Donald, 186
talking to the audience, 40-41
Tap Project, 225
target audiences
  connections, 35
  earning trust, 35
  entertaining
    event sponsorships, 94
    hosting, 92-94
    minglers, 92
  needs, 28-29
  reaching
    depth of knowledge, 30-31
    emotional bonds, 31-32
    functional advantages, 29-30
  relating to, 33
  researching, 160
  talking to, 40-41
Technorati, 193
telephone book advertisements, 152
text messaging, 138-139
thank you's, 89
themes, 226
Toastmasters International, 83
Todd, Charlie, 224
tone, 212
tools for public relations, 112
  letters/opinion columns, 115
  media advisories, 114-115
  media releases, 112-114
tracking website visitors, 124
trade publications, 102
trademarks, 195
traditional media exposure
  broadcast media, 103
  examples, 100
  print media, 101-102

Tran, Jacquelyn, 193
Trick Dog Gallery, 176
Trump, Donald, 16, 186
trust in target audiences, 35
T-shirt advertisements, 154
T-shirt guerrilla marketing example, 164
Twitter, 129
types of advertising, 148
  airplane banners, 154
  billboards, 154
  broadcast, 148-149
  bumper stickers, 153
  buttons, 153
  direct mail, 152
  endorsements/sponsorships, 153
  newspapers/magazines, 151
  personal letters, 153
  posters, 154
  telephone books, 152
  T-shirts, 154
  webcasts, 149
  websites, 150-151

U–V

U.S. Postal Service websites, 152
upholding reputations, 202

verbal identity, 46-47
viral marketing, 158
Virgin Records, 175
visual identity, 43
vlogs, 131
volunteering, 83

W–X–Y–Z

web
  advantages, 131
  advertising, 150-151
  blogs, 130, 140-142

advertisements, 150-151
posts, 122
conferencing, 143-144
disadvantages, 132
e-mail blasts, 126
electronic newsletters, 125
evolution, 227
example story, 122
personal websites, 123
designing, 123
domain names, 124
search engine optimization, 124
tracking visitors, 124
podcasts, 126-127
social networking, 127
blogs, 130
Facebook, 127-128
Internet forums, 131
LinkedIn, 128
MySpace, 127-128
sites, 140
Twitter, 129
vlogs, 131
YouTube, 129
webcasts, 149
wiki (Wikipedia), 142
Web 2.0, 205
webcasts, 149
websites
advertising, 150-151
Arbitron, 148
Armstrong, Heather B.,
mommy blog, 130
Basic Facts About Trademarks,
195
Career Distinction online identity calculator, 208
extending brands, 176
FactCheck.org, 201
federal trademarks, 195
Nielsen, 148
ParentTalkToday.com blog, 141

Skype, 143
U.S. Postal Service, 152
wiki (Wikipedia), 142
weekly newspapers, 101
Western traditions with different
international meanings, 197-198
Wexner, Les, 10
white space, 45
Wieden, Dan, 7
wiki (Wikipedia), 142
wild posting campaigns, 159
Winfrey, Oprah
beginning her brand, 41
reputation, 16
women's clothing, 86
Woods, Tiger, 182
word of mouth guerrilla marketing, 162
workplace associations, 79
World Is Flat, The, 190
world's most valuable brands for
2008, 196
worst/best brand extensions, 179
writing
books, 106
columns, 106
personal branding stories
examples, 20
input from others, 20
personal questions, 17
reasons for, 14-15
reflection, 19
reputation, 16-17
statements, 18
summarizing into elevator
pitches, 22

Yo-Yo guerrilla marketing
example, 163
youth sports associations, 82
YouTube, 129

Zuckerberg, Mark, 23

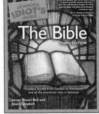